My Journey to Her World

How I Coped with My Wife's Postnatal Depression

by

Michael Lurie

**Grosvenor House
Publishing Limited**

This book is published by
Grosvenor House Publishing Ltd
28-30 High Street, Guildford, Surrey, GU1 3HY.
www.grosvenorhousepublishing.co.uk

A CIP record for this book
is available from the British Library

ISBN 978-1-906210-13-7

To My Worlds:
Kate, Maia and Eden

Foreword

Going through difficult times can either make us stronger or break us.

This book is my story of how I came face-to-face with the devastating illness of depression and in particular postnatal depression, as I witnessed my wife suffer the traumatic effects that victims of this disease are subjected to.

She had suffered from depression before we met and most severely after the birth of our first daughter, which is the first time I experienced its ferocious intensity.

By sharing the story of our relationship from first meeting to present day, I hope to enlighten the reader by offering, unusually, the male perspective on postnatal depression and in a wider context, help sufferers to understand the plight of their partner.

This book is not intended to provoke feelings of pity or sympathy. It is my hope that people in similar situations will be able to relate and identify with these experiences and gain some insight or reflection into their individual encounters.

The complex nature of mental illness and postnatal depression has resulted in it remaining largely misunderstood, stigmatised and hidden from the public gaze. The reality of the experience is seldom shared. Being a male, I found it difficult to express my innermost thoughts. Help in the form of documented experiences was largely unavailable, thus my idea of sharing my own story was born. By doing this, I felt I could help others in similar situations, as well as indulge my own need for emotional release. Cathartic and therapeutic at the time, I hope the underlying sentiments will reach many people, as they largely mirror any encounter with mental illness.

Ultimately, this book is a tribute and salute to my wife for all she has endured. She is the heroine of the story, overcoming adversity and taking control of her destiny without succumbing to a life-long battle with depression. I am immensely proud and honoured to be her husband and could never have married anyone else. I know that whatever challenges lie ahead, we have many years to look forward to. She is my soul mate and my world.

Disclosure

I had just made the most impulsive decision of my life. I was going to live in London. This came as a shock to my family and friends, but more so to myself. I had stepped out of character and decided to take a break from the pressures of my career. The decision was not without influence. My days as a high-flying Marketing Director for an Internet company were drawing to a close. As the 'dot-com bubble' burst, I was brought down a few notches of the corporate ladder and found myself being made redundant.

I was not surprised. I had anticipated the event for many months and considered myself lucky to have survived so long. In some ways, I saw this as a salvation. Here was an opportunity for respite to decide my next move. Fortunately, a good pay-off allowed some time off work in order to do some soul searching.

Being unemployed can have its advantages and I remember feeling relieved, yet somewhat guilty, for not actually having to account to anybody. I was a free man and a master of my own destiny. A sense of empowerment enveloped my mood. I had been given a chance to reflect and perhaps start anew.

My new status in life gave me the opportunity to do something I had neglected for years: socialise and party. I regressed to feeling like a teenager and was aware that the art of socialising for the sake of enjoyment rather than networking for new business, had to be re-learnt. On one cool April evening, I was invited to a birthday party by a good friend who wanted me to meet her rather bohemian social circle. Although I consider myself quite fashionable, I am essentially a conformist at heart. I looked and felt out of place in my Ralph Lauren cords and crisp, white Oxford shirt.

Negative feelings swamped my already self-conscious demeanour as I quickly surmised that this was not my 'scene' at all. The room was dimly lit by heavily scented candles and huge velvet pillows were strewn on the floor. In the background, I could hear the strains of jazz music, which seemed strangely out of place in this decidedly foreign atmosphere. I was sitting opposite an acquaintance whom I recognised to be my friend's flatmate. We started talking as I tried hopelessly to look and feel at ease in this ambience.

She too was unemployed. However, this had been her choice. Her free-spirited nature did not quite allow for working in a conventional job and she preferred an assortment of casual employment, whenever the opportunity arose. We started talking about things we had in common and it transpired that despite our differences, we both shared a passion for travelling. In fact, her plans extended to moving to London for an indefinite period.

London. Great Britain. I had been there several times on business and it had aroused my interest although, in between taxis, airports and meeting rooms, the city itself remained undiscovered. For me, London was symbolic of correctness, conformity and order, all of which I considered to be pillars of stability. The city conjured images of murder-mystery scenes in large Victorian country mansions, red double-decker buses and terribly polite people whose every sentence was interjected by 'sorry' or 'excuse me'.

Yet, as I continued to listen intently to her plans, I was unable to imagine this girl feeling at ease in this culture. I left the 'boho' scene, with the scent of the candles in hot pursuit.

It had been a good day. I was beginning to enjoy my own company again. London. I reflected on the conversation at the party. It seemed inviting. Was this something to consider?

Insomnia seemed to get the better of me. My mind was racing with thoughts on the future and my destiny. By three in the morning, I realised sleep would elude me and decided to surf the Internet to find out more about living in the UK.

By 7am, my decision was made. I was indeed going to London. The finer details of how and why were still not apparent, but the city beckoned me and my instinct told me to go.

I was anxious to share this exciting news. I decided to first tell a very good friend of mine. She was excited by the news and also impressed by my newly found spontaneity.

She told me that if I needed any advice or help, her boyfriend's sister, Kate, who lived in London, would be a good starting point. I took her details and thought little of it.

About a week later, I decided to write to Kate for advice on renting a property. Her email response made an unusual impression on me. I was feeling negative and cynical about relationships at the time, as I had gone through a very traumatic break-up with my girlfriend after a stormy two years. I had been left heartbroken and disillusioned about ever finding the right person. I could not believe in pure love anymore, as I saw it as all consuming and potentially destructive. My guard was up and my vulnerability prevented me from wanting to take the risk of another failed relationship.

A move to London had appealed initially as it allowed me to escape from albeit well -meaning friends intent on finding me suitors, as well as offering me the opportunity to rediscover my bachelorhood.

Kate had managed to tear down my guard in a few lines of an email. Her tone and writing style brought a wide smile to my face. She was the antithesis of my ex: so warm, reassuring and good hearted. I desperately needed this, but decided that my imagination had run away with me and that she was probably only being polite with no hidden agenda.

July 12th 2001.

London

Our first meeting.

We had agreed to meet at a coffee shop. I had a vague impression of her appearance from a photo I had seen, but, as I stood outside waiting for her, a sensation of butterflies in my stomach engulfed me, even though this was not a date, but a friendly meeting. We had talked several times on the telephone prior to my arrival in London and it seemed as if we had known each other for a long time.

As I looked through the window of the coffee shop, I felt a hand gently touching my back. A very tall, slim and unusually beautiful woman was smiling at me. Her turquoise eyes penetrated me like an X-ray machine and I suddenly felt emotionally transparent.

We chatted about employment prospects and other issues concerning a newcomer, but all was lost in the heady warmth of the sensation inside my chest as I was faced with the expansive smile dominating Kate's face. She was the one. I just knew it. I desperately wanted to share my feelings there and then but my sense of reason prevailed.

I was the new boy in town. I knew nobody apart from Kate and the bohemian at the birthday party. I was reluctant to take this introduction further for fear of rejection and I wanted my entrance onto a new social circuit to remain unblemished.

We finished our meal and Kate offered to give me a lift to my flat. I invited her in to look at my CV. We seemed very comfortable in each other's company. Kate was classically beautiful, yet seemingly unaware of it, which enhanced her appeal. My hermetically-sealed defence mechanisms seemed to burst open. Until now, I had avoided the possibility of rejection. The moment had changed it all.

The next day I decided to tell her. I was tired of playing relationship games and wanted to be true to my honest, direct nature.

"I like you more than just a friend. Would you like to go out on a date?" My enthusiasm was reciprocated. Several months later, as we reflected on this moment, we realised that we had both been feeling the same way from the outset.

The next few weeks were pure bliss. I was not due to start my new job for another few weeks, allowing me the opportunity to immerse myself in our relationship. I would wait outside Kate's work most days and walk her home. Our weekends were spent walking in forests and having picnics. This was the honeymoon period of our relationship. The irony of my wanting to progress slowly seemed poignant and even humorous. We were falling deeper in love as every day passed.

One early summer evening, we decided to go for a long, quiet walk in the local park. After a while, we sat down on a bench. In the distance we could see central London, a myriad of buildings and roads, with green stretches of park interspersed.

Silent reflection. Neither of us felt the need to say anything. The setting sufficed. I had found love.

Kate was unusually quiet.

After a few minutes, she distanced herself from me and gave me a serious, pensive look. Something was wrong. "Darling, I have something to tell you." We had referred to each other as 'darling' for some time now and it seemed as natural as ever despite our relationship only spanning a matter of weeks. However this time, the term of endearment seemed paradoxical in light of the formal tone.

I had an awful sense of déjà vu as my previous relationship had ended on such a note. I knew I should not have allowed myself to fall in love again. I was deflated once more and only I was to blame. What had I been thinking? Immersing myself into a deep relationship when I had barely landed in a new country was a huge mistake. I was just waiting to hear the words. It was over.

"I suffer from depression and am on medication", she said. I was dumbfounded, paralysed with shock, yet desperately wanting to convey a nonchalant attitude to the matter. "If you feel you cannot handle this, I understand if you end it now." In what seemed like hours, but was probably no more than a few seconds, I said: "It does not bother me. I love you for the person you are and we will deal with it."

What did I know about depression? What had I just said? Had I meant it? Did I realise what lay ahead? At the time, my love for Kate was absolute and I wanted no barrier to come between us.

Depression. Medication. Images of violent mood swings and visits to psychiatric units suddenly flooded my mind. Prozac. This was the medication of loonies. Normal people had no need for this. Kate was absolutely normal, extremely positive and stable. The most shocking thing was that I could not associate my stereotypical views with the person next to me. They just did not match. Depression was akin to mental illness, intangible, stigmatised and misunderstood. I knew nothing of its symptoms and side effects, nor how to detect its advent and how to respond to it.

Silent tears of relief trickled down Kate's rosy cheeks. She had feared that I would not want to pursue the relationship after this revelation. I had feared that it was over. It was not. However, a different reality was present now, a different relationship. Our innocence had been lost. Our honeymoon was over. I had now been introduced to the third partner in our relationship - depression.

We continued to talk and Kate revealed yet more. She had experienced a breakdown a few years earlier following the break up with her fiancé and as a result had been admitted to the Priory Hospital. At the time her engagement broke off, she was living in London and after months of emotional trauma felt unable to continue. Feeling utterly empty inside, and despite her mother coming to care for her, she realised that she had reached a crisis point and needed professional help. In the Priory Hospital she was strongly encouraged to interact in group therapy, as opposed to spending time in solitude and a very strict timetable was in place. She related the difficulty in getting out of bed every morning to face the nurses with their happy faces, whilst she felt the exact opposite. Although the surroundings were very plush, it had not escaped her notice that the windows did not open more than an inch and there were no locks on the doors.

After hearing about these experiences, I was filled with mixed emotions. My biggest emotion was fear. Could she plunge into another breakdown in the future? Would I be able to cope with it? Would I still love her in this state? Without ever having known her previous fiancé, I felt anger towards him. I simply could not understand how he could have hurt someone he loved in such a way. I wondered what kind of person he must have been to do this. At the same time, a part of me thought that perhaps it was not as black and white as Kate had inferred. After all, every story has two sides.

I was humbled by Kate's experience as it had clearly changed her life. I began to see her in a different light and my respect for her reached even greater heights. I was proud of her for pulling through and having the strength of character to acknowledge the problem.

Kate was a person who had a true life story. She had experienced so much in her short life, moulding her into the person she was. Now, more than ever, I saw her as a survivor. I knew if she could surmount this experience, she certainly had the strength of character to overcome whatever challenges lay ahead. This is what I had always looked for in a partner. I loved her even more as I fully appreciated both her sensitivity and vulnerability, which made her even more endearing.

However, I was yet to fully internalise the impact depression was to have on our relationship.

First Signs

The next few months continued to bring us much happiness. Kate's revelations of her history of depression did not lessen our love and commitment to one another. It simply matured it. We were more measured and thoughtful in our behaviour. Kate felt more comfortable talking to me about her feelings of depression, as and when they occurred. There was no more need for a façade, pretending she was always happy, as she had before.

I felt relieved and happy that we had reached this level of comfort and openness in our relationship, demonstrating our commitment to one another. We realised that our bond had stability and was founded on honesty and awareness.

The word 'depressed' covers a vast array of sentiments. If I say I am 'depressed', medically speaking, I am probably only feeling low. Generally, the word 'depressed' is used rather flippantly and most have no idea of the symptoms a clinically depressed person suffers. Kate sometimes used to say to me: 'I am feeling down.'

'Down' was acceptable and in fact quite normal. I also felt down from time-to-time and this was part of coping with life. One of Kate's misconceptions about those who did not suffer from depression, was the assumption that they were content and happy most of the time. Not so. Most people put on a brave face in public regardless of inner turmoil. Very few people, if any, have no problems at all.

I remember feeling very low for months when my previous relationship came to an end. I felt numb, empty and desolate, but I was determined to carry on my routine and function as normally as possible. Easy it was not. In fact, it was hard just getting up in the morning. Fortunately I needed to earn a living, so I did not have time to hide under the covers. This was a blessing in disguise. Time is a gift, but can also be a burden. We all need time to reflect on personal matters. However, whilst some reflection and introspection is necessary, over analysis and taking a microscopic view of life can be destructive.

However, when one is unable to function on a fundamental level, the situation is more serious. This is when 'down' becomes clinically depressed. I had actually never witnessed Kate's depression first hand. Over the next few months I was to see glimpses of it through small, but significant incidents, which occurred.

Kate had started a new job as an editor for a medical

PR company and although she was enjoying the work itself, was encountering problems with some of her female colleagues. The world of PR is particularly cut-throat and very dominated by ego. Unfortunately, Kate was targeted by over -worked, insecure, aspiring colleagues whose life ambition seemed to be backstabbing each other. Kate is the antithesis of this and found it difficult to deal with the relentless maligning. She just wanted to do her job as best as possible and also enjoy her personal life. This approach was unacceptable to some colleagues however, who felt she needed to be more involved in the corporate culture of the company. Understandably, Kate began feeling the strain and her confidence suffered. Whilst it is entirely to be expected that problems of this type will impact on disposition, I felt Kate was much more affected. I noticed that it was harder for her to go to work every day. I remember her calling me before work to tell me she felt unable to go. I told her to be strong, get out of bed and ignore the people who were making her professional life so miserable. After some persuasion, she finally went, but I knew that her levels of anxiety were on the increase.

When I called her during the day to see how she was, I could sense that despite her best attempts to be strong and positive, she was very down. She started to have a nap in the evenings after work, missing dinner, and I began to be concerned about this behavioural change. This was very unlike her. We were used to eating dinner together every night and I would wait for her outside the tube station to walk back home with her.

When I picked her up one evening, she was visibly drained and had a glazed look on her face. "I am feeling bad about myself. I feel really bad."

I probed her to find out what made her feel bad, but it took a while to discover what was on her mind. Kate struggled to articulate her feelings and eventually I asked her to list her emotions on a piece of paper. Insecure, nervous and guilty. The insecurity stemmed from being afraid that she would not be able to take care of herself and would need to be looked after by someone. The nervousness related to her not being able to cope with looking after herself. Previously, when she was feeling very bad, she had wanted to go to hospital and get a bed where she would feel looked after and secure. The guilt came from not feeling in control of herself, even as an adult.

The events at work had been ongoing for almost a month, with continual persuasion from me to persevere and ride the storm. Every workplace has its politics and unpleasant colleagues, but this was part of life. However, anll was not well with Kate. I decided that we needed a holiday.

Paris

One cannot escape reality, but it sometimes can be put on hold for a short while. This is exactly what we did. We decided to take a long weekend in Paris in order for Kate to see the problems from a different perspective and decide how she wanted to pursue the situation at work. I was very keen on going to Paris as it had a special place in my heart.

I had briefly lived and worked there. It never failed to impress me. On my free evenings, I would walk along the boulevards to the Arc de Triomph and back. I felt as if I were on a continual holiday, living in the midst of this magnificent city which needs no attractions to make it worth visiting. For me, Paris itself was a living museum of culture, romance, history and sophistication.

I enjoyed just wandering about the streets with no clear idea of where I was going. I felt like a child in a sweet shop, unable to decide where to turn next. All roads were appealing.

I was not even envious of the entwined cosmopolitan couples roaming the streets showing clear displays of affection. I was actually happy for them and possibly experienced love vicariously. It was not my time yet.

Whilst I mostly enjoyed my own company, I distinctly remember an occasion where I was engulfed by a sense of profound loneliness and isolation. I had come back to my hotel after a stressful day at work and decided to grab a quick bite and take a brisk walk to the Champs Elysses. It was half an hour's walk from my hotel in the Le Marais quarter.

It was early evening, between dusk and nightfall. I decided to take a rest on a bench by the Louvre to fully appreciate the moment. I sat down, mesmerised by the view.

It was breathtaking. The dim lights of an amusement park were shimmering in the background. I could hear the sounds of a concertina emanating from a street performer. The shadows of the monumental buildings around me increased the sense of awe. I could almost hear and see the last century of history unfold in front of me. As it was an autumn evening, the naked trees provided a stark, if not sad, contrast to the bright lights in the background. Very few people were around and I had time to reflect.

Quite suddenly, I felt a swelling sensation rise from my gut to my eyes. I was trembling and holding back tears. I had never felt so lonely in all my life. Here I was in this beautiful setting, but could not share the moment with anyone I knew or cared for. I became acutely aware of the missing element in my life, companionship.

I decided that our weekend in Paris would be an opportunity to lay those feelings of desperate loneliness to rest and give me the closure I needed. I would go back to the same spot with Kate. I explained the significance of the location beforehand. When we arrived at the spot, there was no need for words. I had transformed the sad association into a magical moment. Even today, we refer to this spot as our secret 'meeting place'. If we were ever to be apart, we would know where to find each other.

This event gave Kate the opportunity to support me, by filling the vacuum in my life and providing a sense of inner strength. I realised she would also be there for me in times of weakness, and I felt nearer to understanding how isolated a depressed person can feel.

We had a great time in Paris and managed to enjoy the few days together without dwelling too much on the situation at home. There was silent reflection on issues that we discussed at the end of each day, but we did not want to dissect all the aspects of Kate's work on our holiday. We enjoyed each day as it came, strolling through the streets, visiting museums and absorbing the laissez- faire atmosphere Paris had to offer.

Kate seemed to be her usual confident self and had regained her appetite, much to my relief. I knew by now that excessive sleep and lack of appetite were classic signs of depression.

I felt quite pleased with myself, as I thought I had successfully managed to identify the problem and take appropriate action by having a holiday. I was naïve in my judgement. If this was the extent of the depression, I reasoned, I would cope. It was not as bad as I had thought it would be. It was just a matter of picking up the warning signs and dealing with them instantly before they developed into a more serious issue.

I was haunted by these thoughts a year later, when I was given a more realistic dose of the effects of depression.

We were sad to leave Paris, but knew that is was only a couple of hours away if we needed a break.

Back to Reality

Home. We were back in London. For me it was a strange feeling that London was my home. I had only been there for six months, yet I felt settled and at ease. It was not the place itself that made me feel like this. It was Kate. I realised that 'home' was not a physical place. It was an emotional and psychological state of mind, which allowed me to feel at ease with life. My path was inextricably linked with Kate's and it was she who had enabled me to feel at home.

We could have relocated anywhere in the world at that point, but still would have felt at home, because we had each other. This was the stabiliser and rock in our relationship.

We decided to give the situation at Kate's work another month before taking any steps. As it turned out, some of the difficult people left the company a few weeks later. This came as a huge relief, as it meant there was an injection of new people into the company. Kate was pleased at this development and was also glad she had persevered.

She threw herself back into her work and we both seemed to be on track again. Things had stabilised. Our relationship continued to grow and mature and although we had only been together for less than a year, it seemed that we had known each other for much longer. Our courtship was not one of playing ego games. Honesty characterised our union. There would be no unpleasant surprises on the way. I had already met Kate's family and we all got along well from the start. In many ways, Kate's background was similar to mine and I feel this was an important factor in our compatibility. There were similar cultural and life experiences providing a joint frame of reference and familiarity.

We had both been brought up mostly by our mothers. In Kate's instance, her father had tragically died of cancer when she was only eight years old. This left a huge emotional scar that has still never fully healed. In later years, the effects of this tragedy would haunt Kate during her bouts of depression. Barely a week goes by without Kate mentioning the wonderful memories of her father and the sadness of not having had the chance to get to know him better.

In my case, my parents had divorced when I was five. Whilst I had contact with my father after the divorce, the relationship was strained, sporadic and distant. It was my mother who was our anchor in terms of providing stability. For Kate also, it was her mother who had brought up all the children alone and therefore provided the stability. We are fiercely protective of and proud of our mothers, who both overcame such difficult times.

The nurturing we received instilled in us similar values of hard work, honesty and above all, resilience. Our families had been through difficult times, but had overcome the obstacles. Kate and I had a wealth of life experience that had made us stronger as people and acutely aware of the transience of human life.

People cope with life's problems in very different ways. I have never been very good at showing emotion, especially around my family. Perhaps it stems from a sense of vulnerability. During difficult times, I have chosen not to share my feelings, not because I felt they did not care, but because I wanted to deal with problems in my own way. Often, I turn to friends, who are more removed from the situation and can be objective.

When Kate first told me of her depression, I did not say anything to my family. At the time, there were several reasons for this. Firstly, I did not want an interrogation from my mother, especially with regard to the nature of the depression. Coming from a stereotypical society, I knew they probably had old fashioned images of sanatoriums, medication and suicidal tendencies. There had been quite a few people in our community who had suffered from severe depression, some of whom had committed suicide. Unfortunately, depression was one of those unmentionable words like the 'C' word. I also think my family would have worried about how I would cope.

In hindsight, I think I made a mistake by not being more open about it, as it would have mitigated their shock at later events. I also gave them too little credit for being able to understand the condition and I could have attempted to educate them about the illness.

Shortly after Kate told me about her depression, I felt the need to find out more from her mother. Kate's family were different. They had known and experienced her depression for a few years. Whether they accepted it or fully understood it, is another matter altogether. I had the impression that the full extent of the problem was not acknowledged and it was only ever superficially discussed. Kate's mother referred to some of her bouts of depression as 'blips' or 'hiccups' along life's journey.

When I finally brought up the topic with her, I felt she entirely understated it and I tried to understand why this was the case. One reason was possibly because it was something she felt very difficult to come to terms with. She also may have been frightened that it might be too much for me to handle. Moreover, she may have felt that she was in some way responsible for Kate's demeanour, as a result of Kate's difficult childhood. No one could have blamed her though, least of all Kate. I think Kate yearned more than anything for her family to acknowledge the situation. She wanted to be able to be herself and express her feelings, no matter how uneasy it may have made others feel. She simply wanted to talk about her depression without feeling that she was being judged or causing pain or embarrassment. It was and still is, difficult to accept and acknowledge and I think it has taken her family several years to be able to discuss it more openly and frankly.

Planning a Future

As the months passed, it was clear that we needed to discuss our future plans. We had both known from very early on in our relationship that we wanted to build our lives together. Kate felt more strongly about getting married sooner rather than later, as she saw no reason to delay. We were both in love, committed to each other and had been through some trying times, which had strengthened our relationship and reaffirmed its stability and maturity.

On the other hand, I had some reservations that were based on pragmatic considerations. At the time, I was working as a teacher in a high school, unable to find employment in my profession of Marketing, due to visa restrictions. I had come to London wanting to re-train and saw this as part of the new life I was trying to build. I thought it would be more meaningful to teach and would provide me with more job satisfaction than my previous job in the corporate world. I had therefore decided that I would register on a teacher-training scheme, and stay with Kate in the UK, to see how things developed from there.

As it turned out, my experiences of teaching were anything but meaningful and fulfilling. I had expected British children to be well disciplined and responsive to learning, by default. I could not have been more wrong. The level of precociousness and rudeness of some students totally shocked me and I could not believe that children could be so unruly. I had expected a similar level of discipline to that which I had encountered as a child, where respect and good behaviour were the norm. The huge disparity between my expectations and reality left me disillusioned and anxious to resume my career.

At the same time, I felt pessimistic about my earning capacity and felt that I had regressed considerably in my career. I wanted to pursue new job opportunities and stabilise my career before making any marriage commitments. For me, it was inherently wrong to be getting married without having financial stability. I saw it as irresponsible and reckless. However, Kate did not see things in the same way.

She felt that I was waiting for circumstances, which may take a considerable amount of time to come to fruition, and would still never be guaranteed. After all, we knew many people who were in and out of jobs on a regular basis. At the time, there was a huge slump in the general job market due to post 9/11 global economic changes. We had quite a few friends who were being made redundant from very high earning jobs. At least I had a secure job at a school, which would not be compromised by the global economic crises. If anything, it would be strengthened. More than ever, the government sought to improve the educational system and had many incentive schemes for professionals wising to re-train as teachers.

Kate argued that I was in fact more stable in my job than many other people, even if the pay was significantly less than a job in the corporate world. After some convincing, I agreed with her. There was never going to be a perfect time to get married. In the past, when I was most comfortable financially, my social life was practically non-existent, as I was so busy. Now that I had the time to nurture a relationship, I was considerably less solvent than I had hoped.

The terror events in New York and around the world also had a subliminal effect on my change in attitude. I realised that we could spend our lives planning things as we wished them to happen, only to find them totally changed due to events that were out of our control. Kate has a saying that 'man makes plans and G-d laughs'. I came to realise that my natural inclination to be pragmatic and in control was somewhat irrelevant in the wider scheme of things. There were no guarantees of anything in life.

Kate also made it clear that she needed some form of commitment. We both knew people who were in long-term relationships, which had eventually died, without a firm commitment or plan for the future. This had resulted in disillusionment and bitterness, as the emotional investments yielded no return. Kate was not prepared, and would not allow herself, to be one of these people.

After some soul searching, I realised that I needed to be more spontaneous in life and follow my heart. I wanted to, and was going to marry Kate.

The Proposal

I would like to think that I am a romantic of sorts and I was determined make my marriage proposal a truly unforgettable experience. Not for me the glitzy limousine destined for a posh restaurant, with my proposal being witnessed by complete strangers. I wanted the moment I placed a ring on Kate's finger to be a most private experience.

I had a more understated and less orthodox approach in mind. I decided to take Kate on a surprise holiday to a place I had always wanted to visit, Venice.

In my childhood home, an antique painting of Venice hung in our lounge. Elegant gondolas gliding effortlessly on turquoise blue water, surrounded by dome shaped castles in the background, was an image which had stayed with me all my life. I used to sit for hours staring at the painting, almost wishing I was part of it. I had always thought of it as a magical island untouched by the modern world. For me it epitomised romance, charm and ambience.

I had planned the holiday for late April, in the hope that the weather would be pleasant. We were indeed fortunate. The sky and sea were bright explosions of blue and turquoise, enhanced by a warm, penetrating sun. Kate was ecstatic when she finally discovered the destination at the airport check-in desk. Seeing her expansive smile made me feel warm inside and reminded me of the first time I met her. Nothing was more rewarding than seeing Kate happy. I had booked a hotel in the centre of Venice, within walking distance to St Marco Square and the lagoon area.

On our arrival, we were taken aback by the burst of colours around us. Our journey to the hotel on a vaporetto took us past medieval palaces adorning the lagoon area. Each one was unique in its design, colour and appeal and stood regally in the sunlight as we passed by. Unusually, the scene before me looked better in real life than its artistic interpretation. I was now a part of the canvas in my parents' lounge, soaking up the view that had hitherto been only an image.

Kate and I were unified in rapture. This was the perfect setting I had hoped for. I had planned to propose on a gondola on the last night, but the opportunity did not arise. After parting with a substantial amount of money, we found ourselves on a dimly lit gondola in a very secluded area, but in the company of a very commercially minded gondolier. He persisted in interrupting the calm with continual attempts to extend the journey and I was reluctant to have my marriage proposal marred by the zeal of a salesman. The journey, although delightful, was not quite as understated and romantic as we had anticipated, yet we both saw the funny side and had to laugh at the situation.

On the evening of the proposal, I was particularly quiet as we went out for dinner. This was unusual for me, as I tended to be the more garrulous person in the relationship. Kate was quite surprised at my introverted mood and decided to take the lead by telling me where we should go and what we should do, but I wanted her to just relax and go with the flow of the evening. We had some drinks at the Hotel Cipriani, but I could not find the right time to pose the question amidst Kate's interjections.

Eventually, we started heading off towards the Grand Canal to a more isolated area. In the distance was the beautiful Santa Maria della Salute, a magical baroque church standing gracefully at the entrance to the canal. We walked along a peer allowing us to go further into the sea and take a closer look.

As we sat on the warm, wooden beams with our toes in the water, I asked a simple and straightforward question:

"Darling, will you marry me?"

"Of course," was the reply.

We gazed at each other for several minutes without saying anything. Words were superfluous. This was a perfect evening and a perfect memory. We were getting married.

The First Year

October 2002.

After a six-month engagement, we were married in a beautiful ceremony. The wedding took place in an elegant city hall that had been restored to its original glory. The event was relatively small and intimate, but was a natural progression from our engagement setting, in ambience and spirit.

Kate and I had agreed not to see each other during the week before the wedding, as we wanted the week leading up to the ceremony to be filled with anticipation and excitement for our special day. The ceremony was moving and spiritual and the day could not have been more special. Kate looked timeless in a dramatic gold Victorian dress.

As she walked down the aisle, I was yet again in awe of her natural, unassuming beauty to which I had been so drawn from the moment we met. She was truly a unique and wonderful person. Neither of us could have been happier with the long-awaited union. Kate oozed radiance and true happiness. In my wedding speech, I referred to our love for one another as a light in a somewhat dark world. Kate was in many ways a ray of light for me. She made me feel that we were destined to be with one another. We were like two lone stars in a plethora of constellations, which had come together and bonded. Kate was my destiny.

We did not take a honeymoon after the wedding, as we were both starting new jobs. Kate had found a job as a project manager in a health research company. As for me, I had still not managed to find anything in my profession of Marketing, as my visa was still not finalised. I did, however, get a job in a special-needs school as a learning-support assistant. Whilst I had loathed my previous teaching job, this new experience proved to be more rewarding and fulfilling than I could have ever imagined. The staff members were extremely supportive and the children were special, in every sense of the word. For the first time in months, I actually enjoyed going to work without counting down the days until the weekend. I put my all into the job and began to see some positive feedback and results for my efforts. The children were responsive and forthcoming and I developed a good rapport with them and my fellow staff. It was satisfying helping others in this way and was exactly what I had been looking for when I left my corporate job, before I met Kate.

My only concern was the salary, which was below my earning capacity, but I decided to work at the school for as long as it took to find a job in my profession. I found it relatively stress-free and because I enjoyed it so much, did not feel the usual strain and fatigue associated with the routine rat-race. Perhaps, in a subliminal way, I almost hoped that it would take me longer to find a new position. I felt very comfortable and settled in this job.

For the first year of our marriage, I remained at the school. It allowed me the time to focus on my marriage without too much additional stress. I was relaxed and at ease with myself. One of the biggest perks of the job was the number of holidays in the year. This gave me a new sense of perspective as I felt that my routine was geared towards the calendar year. I became more aware of the seasons and the circle of life, another reminder of what was really important to me, which provided an even greater sense of protection and stability.

As much as I loved my job, Kate's work experience was not very pleasant. She had to commute into work for over an hour each way and was in a pressurised work environment. Whilst she found the work interesting, the internal politics and disorganisation were very wearing. I felt almost guilty that I was so much happier in my job. I tried to tone down my joy, as I knew that Kate did not need to be reminded of this, although it was obvious to us both that we would be unusually fortunate if we had similarly rewarding employment.

My concern was that Kate's job was beginning to have an impact on her mood and frame of mind. She was constantly tired and suffered erratic sleep patterns. I had visited her work on several occasions and seen first hand the environment she was working in. It was cramped, disorganised and lacked leadership. This was not conducive to a happy workforce.

Kate regularly started coming home late due to pressurised deadlines at work. Whilst this is acceptable from time to time, it started occurring more and more frequently. I could tell that this was something that was not going to improve.

I spent all my spare time applying for jobs in London. However, Kate's sister and her husband were living in Manchester and we went to visit them for the weekend. We were impressed at the considerably slower pace of life and the improved standard of living. London was very expensive and high salaries were necessary to survive. We both needed full-time jobs in order to sustain a relatively comfortable standard of living.

When we came back from our weekend in Manchester, we casually discussed the possibility of looking at job opportunities there and relocating. We decided to do some job searches and see if anything cropped up. Yet our enthusiasm for change was only superficial, as we both knew the difficulties and energies involved in moving. We also had a very diverse social life in London and enjoyed meeting friends on a regular basis.

After a few days, we slipped back into our routines and disregarded the thoughts of a potential move. I did, however, make a resolution to apply for a couple of jobs, to see if anything transpired.

The day after I sent off an application, I was asked for an interview. I was surprised, as I barely remembered applying. I must have submitted my CV for hundreds of jobs in London and literally a handful in Manchester. At first, I did not even think of mentioning it to Kate as it was only a first interview and there was no point in getting our hopes up. It was too early to contemplate change at this premature stage. I have to admit that I was intrigued by the role and also the fact that I had received such a prompt response to my application. The job combined Education and Marketing, two of my passions. I felt that this was an ideal career progression and it would be a rewarding opportunity.

I decided to go for the interview, but only tell Kate about it. She was excited, but agreed that there was no point in getting carried away until something concrete emerged. After two interviews, I was offered the job.

As an initial reaction, I was very flattered by the offer. It resurrected my self-confidence, which had diminished over the past two years and reaffirmed my skills and worth in the job market. However, it also came with reservations on my side about returning to the corporate world. Was this something I wanted to do? I was ambivalent about the situation.

From Kate's point of view, she was keen for us to consider this seriously. This signalled a new start for her too and perhaps an escape from her pressurising work environment. Manchester was also more suited to Kate, as it offered a more provincial, relaxed way of life, which was similar to her upbringing in Scotland.

The next few weeks presented some of the most trying moments in our marriage. If we were ever close to a divorce, this was it.

Something had changed in me. I was not the same person as I had been previously in the corporate world. My values had changed. Now that I finally had the opportunity to return to the corporate world, I was not sure this was what I really wanted to do. I decided to tell my boss at the school about my new job offer and see his response. He was very sad to hear that I was considering leaving and made me a very attractive offer to stay, allowing me to use some of my marketing skills in a higher-level role that would also include some teaching.

I was very torn. I was in the fortunate position to have two attractive job offers and did not know what to do. We were under pressure to make a decision within a few weeks. As Kate and I discussed the advantages and disadvantages of moving, it became clear that we were drifting in opposite directions. Kate wanted a change and I was inclined to stay in London to take up the opportunity of developing professionally in a very rewarding field. I had waited too long to find this kind of work.

Compromise was essential. This is what marriage is about. We decided to ask various family members and friends for advice, but this only increased our confusion.

Our deliberation and indecisiveness led to tension between us. Kate started feeling down again as we had no direction. I knew how critical stability was to her and the past few weeks had ripped it out of her life. She felt confused, unsettled and vulnerable. I was also troubled, but found the period more challenging than anything else. However, I knew that we needed to make a decision as soon as possible.

The stress of the past few weeks culminated in serious anxiety attacks on Kate's part. One evening, as she came in from work, she burst out crying. I had been so absorbed in thinking of the prospects for myself that I had not realised the extent of the pain she was suffering. She had become withdrawn, was not sleeping properly and had the vacant look I had seen before on her face.

We were both concerned about the impact it was having on our relationship. Kate decided to go to her psychiatrist to seek professional help in dealing with the stress and depression she was sinking into. We both went together to hear his advice.

He had worked with Kate in the past and she felt at ease discussing the issues with him. After meeting him, I was equally impressed at his sensitive, non-judgemental approach. He also factored me into the equation and was able to see both arguments. The session brought things to a head, as we had previously agreed to take his advice very seriously.

I had been reminded of the reality I had pushed aside. We all need and crave stability, but, in our case, it was a critical element in Kate's happiness and well-being. Kate also needed to find a job that was more rewarding and less stressful, as her current role was not conducive to a positive frame of mind. This needed to be addressed in the short term, regardless of where we decided to live. The doctor reminded us however, that in life there would always be situations where there is uncertainty and we all need to learn to cope with this. The punch line at the end of the meeting was his final piece of advice, not to move city, as this would be too extreme in the light of the existing situation.

This seemed the way out for us. It provided an end to the indecision. We had been medically advised not to move. Whilst I thought this was a positive development,

Kate still insisted on the move and was determined for us to go and start a new life in Manchester. She was adamant that she would be able to maintain her job by working remotely and occasionally commuting, and was sure we could make it work. She also felt that it was an opportunity for me to get back onto the corporate ladder and give it a final chance before dismissing it. This was an opportunity not to be missed.

I explained my reservations and fears in light of the doctor's advice, but Kate was absolutely convinced that this was the right move and in our best interests. I was overwhelmed by her sense of conviction and for the first time in quite a while, I saw a spark in her that touched me. I could see a fighting spirit in her personality and I was proud of this turnaround. We decided to go.

From the moment we had decided, our plans went into full speed motion. We rented out our flat, packed up our belongings and moved to a rented bungalow. We were sad and slightly apprehensive about leaving all our friends in London. We knew nobody in Manchester, besides Kate's sister and her husband, and this was rather daunting. However, we are both sociable creatures and were fairly confident that we would make friends relatively quickly in our new surroundings.

The excitement of the period was enhanced by Kate's surge of energy and optimism, following our decision to leave London. I was so happy to see the effect it had had on her and felt closer than ever to her. We were focused on the same goals and synchronised in mood. I was reminded of how special Kate was, with her resilience and zest for life.

Something inside me still made me feel uneasy about ignoring the psychiatrist's advice. I tried to rationalise our decision. We were united, and this surely must have counted for more than the doctor's advice. Surely. This decision was to haunt us later in our journey.

Kate had managed to persuade her existing company to allow her to trial a remote working arrangement for a few months. This was good news, as it eased the financial strain on us, with two salaries coming in every month.

We were embarking on the next chapter in our lives, unified as ever and hopeful for the future.

Breaking Down

The first few weeks were blissful in our new home. We arrived in mid-December to be greeted by a blanket of white snow. Our bungalow was cosy and warm and felt like a real family home with its garden and driveway. In London, we had lived in a flat, so this upgrade to a house felt really good. As it was holiday season, we had some time to settle in and have some quality time with each other. We hardly knew anyone, but knew that as long as we had each other's company and support, we would be happy.

My new job was very interesting and I was pleased with the office environment. Everyone was friendly and easy-going. I still had to prove myself, but I saw this as a challenge. Kate was commuting once a week to London and working the rest of the week from home. It seemed to be going well. However, 'seemed' was the operative word.

After about two weeks into her new arrangement, things started to become strained at work. Her manager was off sick with stress for several weeks and consequently, her work was given to Kate, in addition to the regular workload. It was obvious that this was less than optimal. A fortnight of hell followed. The CEO of her company decided that it was his natural right to able to call her at practically any hour of the day at home, demanding she work on an urgent project. Kate began getting calls at the crack of dawn and was being told to work on a project through the night. This was unacceptable. Kate was fatigued and stressed as never before.

To make matters worse, the CEO was verbally abusive towards Kate in one of his fits of anger. I witnessed one of these conversations. I urged Kate to persevere, as it was only a temporary situation, reassuring her that as soon as her manager returned, normality would be resumed. I was tempted to interfere, but decided that this would make Kate appear weak. I pleaded with her to remain calm and not let the pressure get to her. All she could do was her best.

Unfortunately, events took a turn for the worse, and what followed were three of the most difficult months of my life.

In my second week at work, I received a telephone call. A deep howl and whimper echoed on the other end of the line. I was not sure who this was. Was it a prank call? More whimpering. I started to get an uneasy feeling in my gut. After about a minute, I realised that the person on the line was Kate. I had a sick sensation. What had happened? I tried to calm her down and asked her to explain what was wrong. She said: "I can't take it anymore, I can't take it anymore."

There is a procedure in place to deal with the eventuality of a physical trauma, whether as the result of an accident, or not. However, no such procedure exists in the event of a mental breakdown. There is no emergency department to go to, no person to call and nobody qualified to assess state of mind. Kate had suffered a breakdown and only had my help at hand. This gave me a glimpse of the difficulties experienced by mentally ill people. When they are in pain and suffering, who can they turn to? Who do their families turn to? The disparity between society's treatment of the mentally ill and physically ill seemed unfair to me.

It was agonising to feel powerless to help when I heard Kate weeping. Every cell in my body cried with pain for her. I would have paid anything just to be there in those first moments and reassure her that everything was okay. I felt as if my heart had been ripped out with a knife.

I knew it was connected with work and had a strong feeling something had happened. I told Kate to stay where she was and that I would come over as soon as humanly possible. I dashed out of work, after explaining it was an emergency, and got home by taxi as quickly as I could. The journey was only half an hour, yet it felt like hours before I arrived. I eventually found out what had occurred, as Kate explained that she had been personally blamed for a failed project.

I was shocked and livid at what had happened. I decided to call her HR manager for clarification of the situation. I had to be as restrained and civil as possible, but my tone indicated how I felt. I told her in no uncertain terms that Kate's CEO must not, under any circumstances, contact her. I inferred that I would deal with their behaviour at a later stage, but that my first priority was with my wife.

The lady, whom I had met before, was taken aback by my call, but had no words to defend what had happened. I could sense that she knew the matter had been handled in an unacceptable manner.

Kate was huddled on the couch swaying to and fro, mumbling incoherently to herself. When she saw me she could not even get up. All I saw was a pair of bewildered and tormented eyes. The same pair of eyes, which normally glowed and beamed at me, were lifeless.

What had they done to my precious world? I was devastated, but did not show in any way that the situation was out of my control. On the surface, I was fully composed and rational. For the next hour, all I did was hold her tighter than ever without saying much. I wanted her to re-establish her sense of security and let out as much emotion as possible. I had never seen Kate in such a state and I was stunned at her behaviour.

She seemed to have collapsed, like a balloon flying high in the air being abruptly pierced and releasing air in all directions. The next few days were a blur to me.

Kate was a mere shadow of herself and withdrew into her own world. She was scared to be alone and felt vulnerable. She berated herself for making 'mistakes' at work. She blamed herself for everything that had happened. I told her several times that she was not responsible for what had happened. She did not deserve to be spoken to as she had been and had endured emotional and verbal abuse from a senior manager.

The day after the incident occurred, I contacted a solicitor, who advised us how to proceed. Kate did not go back to her work. After several months, we received a formal acknowledgement of their accountability in the incident. However, there was nothing that could compensate for the damage caused by this event.

Kate's confidence had taken a heavy beating and it was several months before she could face a work situation again. What hurt me most was the emotional suffering she endured. She could not sleep for nights on end and was anxious about her future career. She felt violated, betrayed and abused by her previous company.

In some ways, she was angry with herself for giving so much to her work, although she knew there were many people who would not have done so.

Unfortunately, Kate's high level of professionalism and commitment had not been appreciated or valued.

Kate suffered from nightmares for weeks and was clinically depressed. She was unable to get out of bed or perform the most minimal of chores, without being pushed. I was devastated at her fragility and deeply tormented state. Her appetite had also decreased significantly. Every morning, when I went to work, she begged me to stay or allow her to accompany me, as she was terrified of being alone. I wanted to stay home and talk her through her feelings to regain her confidence, but I could not neglect my work indefinitely.

There were days when I was terrified of leaving her alone, as I felt she was not fully lucid. I would ensure that she was either with a friend or family member and told her she could call my work at any time.

Sometimes my rationalising seemed to be no consolation, but I was determined to help Kate to be independent again. I could not protect her from life's realities, but could provide the support she needed. One of my greatest fears was that she may harm herself in desperation. I tried to organise a rota of people who would regularly come over to see her, without her knowing I had asked them to. These people were my silent aides, who guarded and monitored the most precious person in my life. Their loyalty and support helped me to get through each day.

At this point, I felt totally drained. I had just started my new job and was still in my probation period, thus having to give my very best at all times. I chose not to say anything at work about the home situation, as I felt I had not been there long enough to warrant leave. This was my first brush with depression in a more serious form and I was somewhat numbed by the experience.

However, I was more determined than ever that we would get through this period and remained rational and pragmatic. We arranged a daily schedule to help her get on with things without having to dwell on negative thoughts. Kate thrived on routine and was pleased to be active for as long as possible during the day. She also called me several times in the day at work and knew I was always available to talk things through.

There were times when she called and sounded extremely low. Although I wanted to return home to her, I realised that this would ultimately not be of any help, as I could not always be there in a crisis. Kate needed to learn to deal with a problem on her own. I knew from previous experience that she did possess inner strength and resolve and the challenge for both of us was to harness these qualities.

She frequently told me that she did not want to carry on living. She said that she felt like a failure and wanted to die.

I would regularly hear her lament. I was internally

devastated and hurt. How could someone be driven to feel so low? What could I do to help?

We decided to seek professional help with medication and counselling. These were no miracle cures, of course, and the process was more about self-healing and coming to terms with what had happened and ultimately, moving on. We decided to take every day as it came.

Kate's battle was to fight back for her happiness and confidence. It had been ripped away from her in the past few months and she needed to reclaim it. We were fortunate to have a supportive circle of family and friends who helped during this period. The irony is that most people, with the exception of family and very close friends, were totally unaware of Kate's depression. Kate was able to conceal it from the outside world. In many ways, this helped her, as she was forced to forget about her feelings for some of the time and concentrate on living her life.

It was an emotionally and physically exhausting time for us, and by the end of each day, we had little energy left for quality time together. I was not resentful about this, but sad, hurt and angry at the situation. It broke my heart to see Kate suffering and I felt we were engaged in a constant battle against this unwanted partner in our marriage. When I married Kate, I had hoped the depression would take a back seat in our lives.

Unfortunately, we both needed to acknowledge the presence of this partner at various stages, and take control of it, rather than it of us. We needed to be stronger than it. If not, we would lose the battle and our relationship.

Kate found a new job, which appeared to be relatively stress free and her colleagues were very supportive. Her confidence in herself grew once more and she felt more positive.

We had made it through the difficult months with a lot of soul searching and pain, but our relationship had been though a further baptism of fire and we were stronger as a couple.

Pregnancy

The thought of becoming a father was overwhelming. Having come from a family where my parents had divorced when I was five years old, I had not had a constant role model of a father and I was worried that I would be inadequate. From a very early point in our relationship, we discussed having children and were both very clear that this was something we wanted. We decided to wait for at least two years after marrying before even starting to try for a family, allowing us time to build the strong foundations necessary for the advent of children.

After about 18 months of marriage, we felt the time was right. As a precautionary measure and on medical advice, Kate stopped taking her medication while we were trying to conceive.

However, disturbing thoughts were at the back of mind. Would she sink into a depression? Would she be able to cope without medication? How would her moods change?

I was excited, yet apprehensive, at this stage. I knew that pregnancy involved hormonal changes and research indicated that it was impossible to predict what may happen to a sufferer of depression. I had read that many women, who normally suffered from depression, felt a surge of energy and optimism during their pregnancy and were on an emotional high during this time. Also, women with a tendency to depression, were not necessarily doomed to suffer postnatally. This was very encouraging to me.

We decided to take things as they came and not presume the worst case scenario. After a few weeks without medication, Kate seemed surprisingly well. On the whole, life was good. We had settled well into our new surroundings and had a wide social circle. Kate's job was relatively relaxed and she had time to enjoy activities she had neglected in London. For the first time in quite a while, I felt that she was really at peace with herself and perhaps did not need the medication as much as we had thought.

Kate called me up at work one morning and casually told me that we were going to have a baby. At the time, I was in a meeting, and was preoccupied with a report I was working on. When she called me, I failed to pay attention to what she was saying. After a second or two, I replayed the sentence in my head and asked her to repeat it.

Being somewhat of a practical person, I asked her to

tell me how she knew. She said she had taken a home pregnancy test. I was unsure of how accurate these tests were and asked her to make an appointment with her doctor to confirm it. I was so convinced that she was not pregnant, that I distinctly remember continuing my work without even entertaining any thoughts of a baby. The doctor confirmed the pregnancy the next day.

We were ecstatic. I could not concentrate at work for a few days and kept thinking about this exciting development. Kate looked fantastic and had no symptoms of morning sickness or tiredness. In fact, she was literally glowing. We decided not to tell anyone until after the three-month scan, as a precautionary measure.

We were desperate to tell everyone we knew, but were adamant in waiting for the results of the scan. We had heard of stories of miscarriages in the first twelve weeks and did not want to get our hopes up. Endless conversations followed about what we would call the baby and how we would raise it. I would regularly kiss Kate's tummy and talk to the baby. We beamed at each other with happiness. This was truly wonderful.

I was still amazed at Kate's positive frame of mind and had a feeling that all would be well. She told me that the pregnancy made her feel protected from the depression, as if the baby was protecting her. Finally, after the results of the scan, we told our family and friends who were absolutely delighted at the news. This was a first grandchild on both sides and there was no doubt this baby was going to be very loved and wanted.

We felt a huge sense of relief after we told everyone as it allowed us to share our thoughts and feelings without having to keep it all to ourselves.

One day, Kate woke up and told me that she did not want the baby. I was shocked, yet dismissive of the comment. Towards the end of the seventh month of the pregnancy, Kate had been through a difficult few weeks where she had intense abdominal pain. We went to the hospital several times, only to be assured it was nothing to worry about. The baby had apparently been stretching itself in the womb with little understanding of the pain it was causing. When we came back from the hospital on one occasion, Kate told me again and again that she did not want the baby.

At the time, I thought it was a reactive comment to a pressurised few weeks and that it was not a forewarning of something worse. After some lengthy discussions, I convinced Kate that she was just feeling naturally low and was not showing signs of depression. Looking back, I was probably trying to convince myself that it was just a 'one-off', but now I admit that as a husband and father-to-be, I was probably in denial or too immersed in my own excitement of the birth of the baby. Several months down the line, I apologised for not having taken this as seriously as I should have. In hindsight, I still have a sense of guilt for perhaps not allowing Kate to feel comfortable to express her sadness or depression during the pregnancy. I think she suppressed some of these feelings for fear of making me feel that she was ungrateful or unappreciative of the relatively easy pregnancy.

Two days after the due date, reality slapped us in hard in the face. Kate had been feeling down over the last few weeks. There were no signs of the baby arriving and it seemed she would be overdue. We were assured by friends that this was normal, especially for a first child. I thought it understandable that she felt down, as it was a very frustrating situation to be in. I advised her to mention it to the doctor when she went for her final check up.

A few hours later, I got a call at work. Kate was crying hysterically. Something had happened. Had she lost the baby? Terrible thoughts raced through my mind as I tried to maintain my composure. After a few minutes, I managed to calm her down and find out what had happened.

Kate had told her doctor that she was feeling low and he responded by saying that she 'was making a mountain out of a molehill.' As it happened, the doctor had seen us at a wedding the week before, and during his consultation, he had the audacity to comment that he had seen her dancing at the wedding and she had seemed fine to him.

I was livid. How could he have made such a reckless, irresponsible and unprofessional comment? This was exacerbated by the fact that he was fully aware of Kate's history of depression.

I eventually managed to calm her down and rushed back home to sort out the problem. After a very heated discussion with the doctor, he retracted his words, but did not fully apologise. We immediately changed doctors.

This incident made me realise the importance of finding a doctor who is receptive and sensitive to the area of mental illness. Not all doctors possess the capacity or tolerance to treat mental and physical illness with the same level of concern and this is a significant shortcoming of the public health system. This particular doctor was not adequately trained or attuned to identify Kate's symptoms and refer her to a specialist for treatment. His combined misjudgement, along with gross insensitivity could have had disastrous effects on our lives.

This incident was a wake-up call. I had been in denial for several months and Kate was not okay. She was extremely fragile and vulnerable and needed some help. I realised the importance of being there to support her and was horrified to imagine how she would be without such support. It was unthinkable.

I talked about this with the doctor. He agreed that

the impact of words on a person suffering from depression is huge. Moreover, I realised the need to be aware of cries for help and not to underestimate the pain felt by sufferers. Many times, a person simply needs someone to acknowledge the pain and affirm that it is legitimate. Having the answer to the pain is of secondary importance. In many instances, there is no short-term answer.

Birth

23rd April 2005.

The birth of our darling daughter Maia Hettie.

She finally arrived 16 days after the due date. Kate had been booked in for an induction, which was delayed by two days, due to staff shortages.

Eventually, on Friday night at 5pm, nature was given a quick start and the proceedings began. We had been through a hellish couple of days not knowing when labour would start. The waiting and uncertainty was not helpful to Kate's already fragile state of mind and made her feel low. However, as soon as we knew it was going to happen, we were rushed upstairs to the delivery suite and a sense of huge relief and excitement overcame us.

The labour was relatively pain free and lasted 17 hours. As she was born, we heard a loud, yet unbelievably comforting cry, which resonated around the room. My biggest fear had been a still-birth and we both heaved a sigh of relief.

As the umbilical cord was cut, she was put in my arms and wrapped up in a green hospital sheet. We specifically asked not to be told the sex of the baby as we wanted to find out together.

At this stage, I was still numb from joy and shock. I brought the baby to Kate and together we unwrapped her to discover she was a girl. Another lady in my life. At first, I had secretly hoped for a boy, but from the time I laid eyes on this miracle, I could not have wished for anything other than Maia. I was given the honour of being the first person to dress her, trembling as I clumsily attempted to put her tiny arms and legs through the holes of the vest. As I dressed her, I thought of how dependent this baby was on us. Maia's skin was covered in a white protective layer called the vernix, which is nature's version of a moisturiser. We were told not to wipe it off, but rather let it absorb into the skin. I shall never forget the smell. The protective coating had a milk-like fragrance and I could not stop inhaling it. I wished she would always have this layer protecting her from life as she grew up. Instead, I knew she would have to build her own defence mechanisms.

She was perfect and looked like her mother. Life changed from that moment on and we now had to share our love for our daughter. Whilst this is seemingly obvious and natural, it posed and to some extent still does pose, one of the greatest challenges in a relationship. The transition from being a couple to being parents was somewhat overwhelming at the time. During the pregnancy, Kate had expressed concern about shared attention and love with a new baby. Despite my continual assurances, I think this still bothered her.

Kate's feelings, when Maia was born, were totally different to mine. She cried whilst Maia was screaming. One of Kate's overriding memories was of Maia screaming for two whole hours, from 10am till 12 noon. She recalled the image of a red, furious baby, angry to have been finally taken from her peaceful world and placed into ours. As I lovingly kissed Maia, Kate later told me that she could not understand what I was doing as she had felt no desire whatsoever to do this. It was the last thing she thought of doing.

The next few hours were surreal. We stared at our creation and could not comprehend that she was our child. Parenthood had descended upon us and we were numb with excitement. It was a combination of fear, awe and sheer joy.

The family arrived at exactly 2pm, the earliest possible time after the birth due to the hospital's strict visiting hours. Flowers, card and fuzzy toys surrounded Kate's bed. We were in a bubble of innocence and detached from reality. It was purely magical. Kate was visibly exhausted and quite subdued, but had an internal glow of happiness. I loved and appreciated her more than ever for everything she had been through. I also realised what an easy job we, as men, have in the birth process.

As visiting hours were coming to an end, I was allowed to spend some extra time with Kate and the baby. It gave us some time for silent reflection.

Finally, when it was time to go, I bent over to kiss Maia, and my eyes made contact with Kate who had the most terrified look I had ever seen. Without uttering a word, I had the strongest feeling I knew what she was thinking. After what seemed like hours, but was probably only a few seconds, Kate pleaded with me not to leave.

I reassured her in a somewhat flippant manner that I would only be gone until the morning. I really had to go as the midwife was again asking me to leave. I gave them both a kiss and walked into the corridor. As I left, I glanced back to wave at my two ladies. I will never forget that moment in all my life. All I could see was a pair of pleading, terrified eyes staring right at me. I knew she was trying to be brave and not say too much. I had seen that look before. This was a cry for help as she felt herself slipping into the dark abyss she had fallen into before, over the last few years. Depression had taken control of the situation once again.

Coming Home

Less than 36 hours after Maia arrived, we were told we could take her home. Kate was attempting to breastfeed, which was proving so much more difficult than we had expected. The hospital was evangelical in its promotion of breastfeeding as the ideal, correct option. The maternity wards were covered in posters depicting glowing mothers with bountiful bosoms breastfeeding their babies effortlessly. What a misrepresentation of the truth! Breastfeeding was a nightmare and despite numerous attempts by midwives, Maia was not interested.

Kate was desperate to leave hospital. She hated being alone there at night, both before Maia was born and after. Beforehand, she was on a mixed ante and postnatal ward with one other pregnant lady who had gone into premature labour, and two other women who had given birth. The ward was overheated, stuffy, and smelly. An artificial light remained on throughout the night and this added to Kate's restlessness, as the days and nights merged into one span of time. Kate told me that there was a new mother on the ward who was snoring so loudly that she could still hear her whilst wearing earplugs. Her baby cried all night, but the mother was oblivious.

As Maia continued to struggle with breastfeeding, Kate felt more and more anxious, which further increased her feelings of depression. She had been a mother for less than two days and was already being made to feel inadequate.

I, like many others, had been brainwashed into seeing breastfeeding as optimal at all costs and throughout the pregnancy had pushed for this as the preferred method. In retrospect, I should have reassured Kate that bottle-feeding was more than fine, if it felt easier for her.

It is very important for a new mother to feel adequate and confident in her ability to be a good parent. Breastfeeding was not for Kate or Maia. We should have accepted this at an earlier stage and looked at other options. Unfortunately, on advice from others and due to inexperience on our part, we persevered for almost two weeks.

Kate's difficulty with breastfeeding may well have been ameliorated if she had been given adequate support and guidance from the midwives at the hospital. Unfortunately, they were seriously overworked and the ward was understaffed. On a ward of about 20 women, there were only three midwives, who did not have the time to provide help with breastfeeding. I think the difficulties Kate encountered trying to do something so seemingly natural, acted as a catalyst in the progressive deterioration, which was to follow over the next few months.

We dressed and bathed Maia before leaving the hospital. We still had not fully internalised the events of the last 36 hours. This precious angel dressed in white was coming home with us and we would start the process of being her carers for the rest of her life. It was overwhelming. Although Kate was happy to be going home to familiar, warmer surroundings, I knew she was frightened of how we would cope. What would we do with this baby when we got home? I could still see the glazed look on Kate's face as we packed up our belongings. She was very distant.

I kept on saying to myself that she was exhausted and overwhelmed and probably had the 'baby blues'. I did not want to accept that this could be more serious. I did not have the energy to deal with that now. I just wanted to enjoy these precious moments of being a new father, so vividly described in the baby books.

The journey home was silent and reflective. We were still absorbing the reality of what was happening. We had been in a vacuum for the last four days and had forgotten that life had carried on around us. The traffic jams were still there, as was the homeless person in the park near our house. We had just added another human being to this reality. The challenge ahead of us was how to integrate Maia into our world, without substituting the reality we had come to know, with something unrecognisable.

As we walked into our house it looked just as we left it before going to the hospital. I closed the door behind us.

Silence.

Home at last.

The First Days

From the moment we got home from the hospital, we seemed to be on a constant treadmill without any option of adjusting its speed or intensity.

Cards, balloons, flowers, toys, clothes, food, messages and visits. We were surrounded by these tokens of joy from friends and family wishing to share this milestone with us. Kate's mother had moved in to help us with the baby. I was happy with this as we got along well in the past and I knew that she would be a proactive, practical support. It also allowed me to go back to work after two days and Kate would have help on hand.

We both felt that we needed to introduce an element of control into this new reality. During the pregnancy, we had researched the various approaches to looking after newborns and had decided to adopt the routine approach propagated by Gina Ford. The issue of a schedule was of particular importance to us, as I knew that Kate was the kind of person who needed and thrived on a timetable to give her a sense of stability and direction.

Naturally we were both exhausted, both mentally and physically. Maia was a very easy-going baby from birth, and in relative terms was a dream baby. However, she still needed constant nurturing and slept for no longer than a couple of hours at a time. We decided to keep her in a Moses basket next to our bed, in order to be as accessible as possible but it proved very difficult for us to switch off, even when she fell asleep. We were still at the 'neurotic' stage where every delicate sigh, breath or movement alerted us and made us check to see if she was okay.

Sleep depravation is detrimental at the best of times. If you are feeling low and recovering from childbirth, it can make you physically ill. As Kate was still breastfeeding at the time, there was not much I could do during feeds. I was also back at work, so had to have some hours of sleep in order to function. I watched Kate sitting on the nursing chair and trying so hard to get Maia to feed. Whilst she did feed initially, it was by no means enough for Maia and it was painstakingly slow.

The next day, the midwife advised us to express milk and drip feed Maia with a syringe. We still wanted to attempt breastfeeding and wanted to avoid nipple-teat confusion. This sounded like a good idea as it allowed Kate to rest whilst I did some night feeds. We tried this method for a few days. I felt it almost demeaning to Maia to be fed the best of Mother Nature's milk through a syringe, which was so clinical. Why could it not be the bonding experience we were hoping for? We were bitterly disappointed.

As the stream of visitors descended upon our home, Kate was still able to project a sense of control of the situation and most people would have thought she was at most a little tired, but definitely not depressed.

Covering up. This is an art, which Kate had mastered. Most people would never have known that anything was wrong in the first few days after Maia's birth. She felt obligated to show the world how thrilled and honoured she was with her new status, how everything was in control and what a competent mother and wife she was.

This noble pretence was draining all her energy. By the time I came home from work, I saw the end product. Kate knew that she could have a break from the 'pretence' and could be herself at last.

She broke down, crying that she could not do this anymore. What was I to say to this comment? I tried to reassure her that things would get better and that she was just fatigued and would become more used to the routine. My mother-in-law had also offered to take Maia into her room on alternate nights in order to allow us to sleep. I was also drained. I had made a huge mistake by thinking that I was ready to go back to work after only two days. What had I been thinking?

I have always been a bit of a workaholic and found it difficult to separate business and pleasure. I was under huge pressure at work at the time of the birth and had to train new staff who had joined my team. I felt obliged to ensure their smooth integration into the company and at the same time meet all my deadlines. I did not take into consideration the need to ensure my family's transition to a stable routine. I was too preoccupied with concerns of my work performance as I feared I may under perform and risk losing my job. Being the sole breadwinner of the family placed a huge burden and responsibility on my shoulders and now more than ever, I was aware of the need to provide not only for Kate, but for Maia too. This pressure manifested itself several weeks later.

I invested huge amounts of energy at work for fear of my boss realising I was experiencing difficulties at home. I also used work as an escape from what was emerging as a stormy period. This coping mechanism came at the expense of my home life.

Despite my pressures and responsibilities, I had not factored in the need to be home for the first few weeks. My place was at home with my family. They were my priority. I still feel a sense of guilt and blame myself for not being strong enough to prioritise at the time. However, hindsight is a wonderful gift. At the time, I thought I could juggle my work and home priorities. I was absolutely wrong.

Falling Deeper

Life was becoming a blurred routine for us. We seemed to be constantly feeding, cleaning, and changing with some attempted sleep in between. Luckily, we had a community midwife who came on a daily basis to check up on Kate and the baby. These midwives were our guardian angels who literally saved us from what could have turned out to be a tragic outcome. They were all different from one another, but had one thing in common: experience. They had seen countless examples of postnatally depressed women and alerted us to the problem.

On one particular morning, I happened to be home when the midwife arrived. We were all sitting in the lounge and Kate was feeding Maia breast milk from a syringe. Kate tried desperately to look happy at performing this ritual but we both knew we could not continue like this. The midwife gave a reassuring, but disdainful look at both of us. Without us having to mention it, she said the magic words – it was time to switch to bottle-feeding.

We had been toying with this idea for a few days.

However, guilt and a desire to persevere kept us from stopping. Now, we finally had approval on the authority of an expert and this deflected the need for us to decide. We had to listen to the professional. I was very relieved at this suggestion.

I asked her to scribble down the name of a recommended formula milk and literally rushed out to the local pharmacy to buy the milk, some bottles and a sterilising machine.

I felt like a child who had been given permission to buy his favourite toy and was ecstatic that we could upgrade from a clinical syringe method of feeding, to a proper bottle. It seemed so much more dignified and befitting. I also revelled in the thought that I would also have the opportunity to help with the feeds and bond more with Maia. Kate was relieved as well, as it meant that instead of focusing on the technical aspect of breastfeeding, which had turned into a nightmare, she could actually enjoy the time to nourish Maia and enjoy the experience itself. It also meant that we could ask friends or family to help with the feeding. It was a win-win situation.

I saw this transition to bottle feeding as a turning point and was convinced that it would alleviate a lot of our existing difficulties.

Unfortunately, I overestimated its affect. Whilst it did improve things slightly, Kate's feelings of depression seemed to be intensifying. She was withdrawing more and more into herself and was engaging in minimal communication with her surroundings.

In some ways, the bottle feeding could have made her feel more inadequate as it simply meant that there was one less thing she was required to do. Most of the family were queuing up to feed Maia. At the time, it probably made her feel more alienated from Maia and her surroundings.

When I came back one evening, I was greeted by my sister-in-law, who was feeding Maia. Kate was curled up on the couch watching. Kate's sister was very excited at the arrival of her niece and showered Maia with affection. Whilst this was touching and sincere, it made Kate feel even worse, as it seemed to highlight the struggle she was having in bonding with Maia. Kate was comparing herself to her sister and did not understand why she could not be the same with Maia.

I explained that it was different for family and friends. They can easily give a hundred percent attention during the short time they spend with the baby. However, it was impossible for a parent to entertain their children all the time. A child also has to learn to occupy herself and spend time on her own. Whilst this made sense to me, it had little impact on Kate's self esteem.

On one particular visit from the doctor, Kate asked him:

"How will the baby know who her mother is?"

The very essence and wording of the question concerned me greatly as it highlighted Kate's distance from reality. She still could not address Maia by her name and needed to call her a generic term, 'baby'. At the same time, she did not acknowledge that she was the mother. This indicated to me that she had still not come to terms with reality. She was now a mother to a baby called Maia. It would be several weeks before this seemingly obvious sentence was internalised.

Kate felt that everyone except her was cooing in awe over Maia, yet she had no idea of what to say. She was inclined not to talk to Maia but just go through the motions of changing, feeding and bathing her. Babies tend to have quite an intense stare and Maia was no different. Kate was uneasy with this staring as it made her feel like Maia was judging her. Depression made Kate vacant and emotionless.

"I feel like an empty vessel. I have completed my task in life. I have no further purpose. I have had a baby. I am ready for the rubbish bin now."

I would frequently find Kate bending over the crib and crying. She asked me how the baby was going to enjoy life whilst having a depressive mother? She wanted to know what good was she going to be? Was Maia going to be embarrassed about her when she went to school?

My heart broke when I saw this hopeless image of Kate looking so inadequately at Maia. I could not understand Kate's fears of being a dysfunctional mother, as I knew that she would get well and cope extremely well. At the same time, her current frame of mind was so negative that I did have some fears and doubts over whether we would get through it. More than anything, I felt incredible pain and guilt about Kate feeling so little of herself. As tears of helplessness flowed down her sallow cheeks, I yet again felt unable to make her believe it would get better. I too, had no guarantees that things would improve. However, I always had hope.

As Kate's communication levels with the outside world deteriorated, I noticed that family and friends began referring to her in the third person whilst she was in the room. On one occasion, a family member asked how she was feeling today. I was stunned at the question and told them to ask her themselves. One of my biggest concerns and fears was Kate being made to feel that people could not speak to her directly anymore. This tore me apart as I saw it as sign of deterioration in her mood.

When Kate and I have been at the depths of despair in terms of her depression, no matter how difficult the situation has been, I have always insisted on her doing something practical and useful. I never wanted her to feel that she was too dependent on me or that she was incapable of helping herself.

On that same evening, when I clearly saw that Kate was so poorly, I specifically asked her to help with hanging up the washing. I knew she was not really up to offering to do this on her own, but if I asked her, she would agree. After much cajoling, she did help.

Making her help with certain chores to keep her functioning at some level, was one of my coping strategies. I felt I was fire fighting the whole time but was somehow not managing to deal with the causes of the problems. We were providing symptomatic relief to a condition that was getting out of control. I felt that just as we made some progress, we were sucked back into the hole of desperation. Things were getting worse.

Insects

"I've got insects. Help me to get rid of the insects!", Kate whispered to me, gradually getting louder. Kate said it over and over again like a mantra. Insects, insects, insects. The first time I heard this, I did not quite understand what it meant.

Brown, hairy, multi-legged creatures protected by a shiny shell. That is how she described them when I asked her. She said that they made her panic. I never thought of other associations for these rather unpleasant crustaceans. For Kate, insects had far more malignant associations. Kate's feelings of anxiety and depression manifested themselves inside her body as insects. When she was particularly down, she felt a sick sensation of insects crawling up her oesophagus to other parts of her body.

This was a warning bell to the worsening situation. When Kate had suffered previous bouts of depression, she had felt these insects and I knew that the situation was serious.

Kate begged me to get rid of them. How could I eradicate these feelings, which were so real and almost tangible? How were we going to alleviate this acute pain? I felt absolutely helpless and useless. No amount of rationalising these feelings was going to be of use at the time. Kate pleaded with me not to tell anyone about these 'insects' for fear that they thought she was really 'losing it'. She told me that she was scared that people would think she was a lunatic.

When I first heard about these 'insects' I too was alarmed. I tried to compare them to what we would call 'butterflies'. I tried to placate Kate and told her that we all suffered from time to time with insects or butterflies and that this was normal, especially in her current frame of mind. Yet again, I underestimated the importance of this behaviour.

As I returned home from work one day, I saw a sight I will never forget. I came into the bedroom and saw Kate sitting on the bed with her back facing me. As I approached her from behind to give her a hug, I saw that she was scratching her neck area with an increasing intensity. At first I thought she just had an itch, but as I looked close, I saw that her throat was marked with scratches from what had seemingly been a prolonged period of scratching.

My gut feeling told me something was definitely wrong. As I looked at Kate, I saw a combined expression of torment, anxiety and physical pain.

Before I could even say anything or ask what was wrong, she said:

"The insects can't get out. They are stuck. They need to get out!"

I could not even begin to understand how this must have felt for Kate. My head just raced with thoughts on how torturous this must have been for her. At the same time, I was so scared that she might have seriously hurt herself if I would have come home later. Yet again, I felt hopeless at being able to predict the situation and felt totally ignorant about the symptoms of the depression.

My initial response was my standard one. I simply held her tight and reassured her that I would do my best to help get rid of them.

"Please tell the insects to go away. Please! I cannot stand this anymore!"

What could I say to such a request? This was something that was clearly not within my expertise and I was not equipped to deal with it. We needed further urgent medical help.

We had to 'up the ante' and get further medical advice. We made an appointment with the GP. When I explained the incident of the insects, the doctor indicated that this was an indication of a more severe form of depression and that these insects were some form of hallucination. Whilst this was an indication of an escalation of the problem, the doctor also reassured me that this was a normal symptom of people in a similar situation to Kate. I was starting to wonder what 'normal' really was.

In some ways, this did reassure me, but at the same time left me in more of a panic about what else could possibly be in store for us.

Several months later, I shared my feelings with a work colleague who herself suffered from depression. I showed her some of the thoughts I had articulated onto paper. When she read about the insects, she started crying. I was quite surprised by her response and curious as to what had caused this reaction. She told me that her tears were tears of relief as she had experienced similar symptoms throughout her years of depression. She too had felt it bizarre and did not think there was anyone else who could have experienced something like that.

I felt as if we were on a roller coaster and had no idea of its duration or path and this scared me more than anything. If I could have known beforehand about the possible situations we would face, I might have been better prepared to deal with the problems we had. At no stage before or after the birth was there any mention of what was likely to happen. I felt that the response from the professionals was more reactive than proactive. We always seemed to be one step behind the illness. My insides were screaming for more information and guidance from them. I needed a roadmap to keep me going. Unfortunately, I was left to my own devices.

The doctor prescribed Kate with anti depressants. The only problem was that these would take at least two weeks to have any effect, whilst the medication was absorbed by the body. Two weeks was an eternity. How would we cope until then? What if things got worse? What if the medication failed to help?

I realise now that medication was not the only answer to the depression. Whilst it may take the edge off some of the symptoms, there is no miracle cure for this illness. It requires a multi-pronged approach that addresses the causes of the depression and provides practical solutions to the problems. We had to make it through the next few weeks and ride the storm until the medication got to work.

Even today, Kate sometimes experiences a sensation of insects, albeit in a much milder form. We now know how to deal with this issue in its early stages and resolve the situation by talking about the causes of the insects. In most cases, we are able to eradicate them.

We recently celebrated our wedding anniversary and I decided to get Kate a necklace with a pendant on it. I asked her to think of it as a reminder of Maia and I and at the same time to remember that whenever she felt the sensation of insects or other negative thoughts, all she needed to do was to hold the pendant and remember that she was not alone. Whilst this may seem childish to some, it has given reassurance to her about being fully supported and loved. I too have my own 'pendant' at work in the form of a framed photo of Kate and Maia. Whenever I am stressed or feel that things are trying, I look at the photo and it puts things into perspective. Ultimately, we all need something to keep us going when things are difficult. Whether it is a pendant, a photo or just a thought, all these things are legitimate and justified.

Mothers

There is a saying that when a daughter marries, her parents gain a son-in-law, but when a son marries, the parents lose him to his new wife. At times I wondered about this saying and thought it to be untrue for the most part. I am lucky to enjoy a very close relationship with my mother and an indebted to her for my solid upbringing. As we lived in different countries, she had only met Kate on a few occasions, for no more than a couple of days at a time.

It is probably fair to say that they were relative strangers. We had arranged for Kate's mother to come to stay with us immediately after the birth for a couple of weeks and thought it advisable to invite my mother separately, shortly after, in order to have more help over a longer period of time.

When we made this arrangement however, we had not anticipated that Kate would be feeling down, but all the travel arrangements were in place for my mother, who was coming from overseas.

Kate expressed some concern about her arrival, feeling that she may be uncomfortable around her in her depressed state. I felt ambivalent about this, realising that on one hand, I wanted my mother to be with us to provide practical and moral support, but on the other hand, I understood Kate's reservations. The matter was further complicated as, naturally, my mother was desperate to see her grandchild. I also wanted the support of someone on my side of the family, and wanted them to be equally involved in this most happy event. Truthfully, I was also needy of moral support during this difficult time and I had on occasions, felt sidelined.

However, I understood Kate's desire to feel she could be relaxed at home, without having to stand on ceremony in front of guests. I knew that she was nervous about my mother's impending visit. She said that she had no idea how she was going to be emotionally and physically and although she could shout and scream at her mother quite openly, she felt she would have to unnaturally control her feelings in front of mine. I tried to put aside my feelings of resentment about this, as Kate was depressed and this was not the time for debate.

Ultimately, we decided to go ahead with the original plan, as it was too late to be altered. However, I felt it necessary to forewarn my mother about the situation.

When I collected her a few days later from the airport, her joy was immediately evident and she was anxious indeed to see her grandchild for the first time.

When we finally arrived home, Kate was in bed trying to escape the world by hiding under her duvet. This was the only place she felt safe these days. She was not on top form to greet my mother. I took Maia out of her crib and introduced her to her grandmother. It was an emotional moment and one that my mother had awaited for a long time. A first grandchild.

Then I approached Kate in bed. She looked so dishevelled in comparison to my smartly dressed mother. My mother had a beaming smile on her face and Kate only managed a very weak 'hello' before disappearing under the covers again. She felt awkward and I could see that it was a strain on her.

It took some time to coax Kate out of bed and get her dressed. She would stay in her pyjamas all day if she could, but I made a point of calling her from work each day to make sure she was dressed. Kate looked frightened as she listened to my mother cooing over Maia. I could tell that she was scared that someone else had entered her cocoon. She just did not want to go downstairs and face someone new. I managed to strike a deal with her in order to get her out of her room.

I cajoled her into going shopping in order to give her a break from Maia and the home surroundings. We went to the local shopping mall. Every step Kate took seemed to require so much effort and I could sense that she was in a worse state than earlier on in the day. Progress was painfully slow as I coaxed her along step by step. I asked if she felt comfortable about my mother's visit, and she said it was fine.

Unfortunately, that was not the case. As we entered the driveway and were about to enter the house, Kate fell apart. She was screaming.

"I want my mummy! I want my mummy! I don't want to go home! Please don't make me go in". I bargained and begged her, but to no avail.

I was speechless, confused and slightly offended all at once. Why was this happening today of all days? My mother had only just arrived and I wanted her to feel welcome and enjoy this period. Why should she be deprived of that? My mother had a right to be there. It was her son and grandchild's lives as well. On the other hand, Kate was my wife, my soul mate. I needed to be sensitive to her needs and frame of mind. I felt torn between my roles as a husband, father and son.

I was stunned at the magnitude of the wailing. I had never seen Kate in such a state and it seemed infinitely worse than previous episodes of depression. This outburst was heart wrenching. All my efforts to console her were futile. The crying only got louder and so intense that she could not breathe properly. She started to hyperventilate – I just had to calm her down. I had the feeling that she would rather die than go back in. She told me that she just wanted the world to swallow her up. At that moment, I felt that I needed to make alternative arrangements for my mother. Yet, at the same time, felt I would not be able to manage without her.

What could I do? I decided to let her 'get it all out' before trying to speak about it. It was clear that there was much going on inside. I held her in my arms for some time until the tears and pain seemed to subside. It was as if she had regressed to being a child and eventually I managed to lead her back into the house. I kept on asking myself what had I done to cause this situation? How could someone I loved so much feel so unhappy? Why was I unable to make things better? Why did Kate need her mommy and not me?

When we came into the house, my mother could see that something was wrong. I gestured to her that Kate was not well and we went upstairs to talk. As Kate lay on the bed, she broke down once again and started screaming for help. It was soul destroying to witness and feel so helpless. I kept on asking myself what I could do to make this go away. I wished I could take away some of the pain. One of the most frustrating aspects of depression is its invisibility. Physical ailments are more easily understood, are tangible and can often be treated. Patients are able to see their progress, as can their family and friends. Mental illness is very different.

We are often unaware of the silent suffering of these patients and treatment is more complex.

The timing of my mother's arrival could not have been worse. She was visibly shocked at how poorly Kate was, as was I, to some extent. If I could have known that Kate would be so down, I would have told my mother to postpone the visit. I think Kate was shocked herself at her condition. Prior to the visit she had tried to be positive about it, but her depression got the better of her. I think my mother also felt she had not been given an accurate picture of the situation, which made her feel less able to provide support. I did not want to involve too many people, thinking that we should deal with the problem as a couple, but I was mistaken. This approach was wrong. My family needed to know and would have reacted differently if I had prepared them beforehand.

Rock Bottom

The next few hours were like hell on earth. Kate plunged to her lowest point ever.

"I want to die. I cannot continue. Let me die. I just cannot go on like this." She told me how, since Maia was born, she felt more in touch with her mortality. Before the birth she was someone's child and now she was someone's mother. Now she had reproduced, she had completed her purpose in life and was ready to let go. Maybe this feeling had something to do with her father dying when she was just the tender age of eight.

She told me that she had reached parenthood without any fillings in her teeth and now it did not matter if she had any – it was a milestone for her and now that she had reached it, there was no reason to continue. I wondered if other first-time mothers felt the same way.

In some ways, I could understand this rationale. Until becoming a husband and then a parent, I had never paid too much attention to my mortality or life's transience, as no-one's future depended directly on mine. On reflection, it is daunting to know that others depend on me, but at the same time, I remind myself that over thousands of years, mankind has continued due to procreation and people manage in some way or another.

I realise now the enormity of bringing up children and see my parents in a different light altogether. I have become aware of the aging process, and the passage of time.

The anguish and torment I felt when Kate uttered those words were bewildering. I hugged her as she wept and cried. I simply could not imagine life without her. I wanted someone to tell me how this could be happening. Every word was another hard blow to my face. I was heartbroken. How could someone so beautiful, with so much to live for, think so little of herself and her future? How could someone feel so low that they see no point in continuing to live?

I managed to respond with some words of comfort and asked her if she really wanted to leave her world of family and friends. The answer was 'yes'. I repeated the question, hoping that I had misheard.

"I want to die. I cannot live anymore."

We were at ground zero.

How could I respond to a comment like this? For the first time during our relationship of almost five years, I felt I had lost her. The 'third partner' in our marriage had managed to snatch away the love of my life with its claws. My attempts to overcome this struggle had failed. I was speechless and numb with pain. Kate looked and acted like an empty vessel. On the surface she was there, but could not have been more distant in spirit. She too seemed to have succumbed.

After a few minutes of shock, my thoughts reverted to reason. This was not Kate talking. Depression had robbed her of rational thoughts and she was not in control of her actions. I was frightened for her and for us, but my heart and head told me I had to stay strong to keep us afloat. I could not project my feelings of helplessness, despair and fear. Kate and Maia needed me.

Internally, my mind was racing with thoughts of terrible outcomes to the situation we were in. As much I did not want to entertain negative thoughts, it was impossible to keep them at bay.

On some of the sleepless nights, I had thoughts of losing Kate. What would happen if she really did try to end things? How could I protect her from feeling this way? What guarantees were there that we would weather the storm? I felt we were barely managing to keep it together. I hated myself for having such cynical thoughts. I had a recurring image in my mind of someone telling me that Kate was gone and I could almost feel the loss as if it was real. It made me scream inside. I prayed to G-d to let her get better and give me the tools to help her. I was too ashamed to share these morbid thoughts with anyone. I also could not believe it had come to this. I was terrified.

As I lay in bed thinking of what would be, I began to wonder how many other men were in a similar situation and how they had coped. On occasions, I thought that perhaps there was something wrong with me and that other men just got on with it. Maybe I was weak and needed to toughen up. My instincts told me however, that this was not merely weakness of character. I was suffering an indescribable ordeal, which no one could really understand unless they had experienced it themselves. There must be others in the same boat, lying awake, without any help or guidance. There must be...

Throughout these immensely trying times, I never had any doubts about our love and commitment to one another. They were not at risk of corroding. If anything, this experience made me love and cherish Kate even more as I knew that we were fighting to keep our life and future together, which inextricably linked us. My thoughts were about ensuring that nothing happened to uproot our lives. I just could not imagine living without my Kate.

We called the doctor, who was very concerned about the turn of events. He immediately increased the dosage of medication and sent a community mental health nurse to come and visit. She diagnosed what we knew was already the problem and confirmed that this was a very serious case of depression that would need to be monitored. It was illuminating to learn about the health system and the way it deals with mental health. In order to be urgently referred to a mental health worker, a patient needs to be in a very severe state.

We were told by the visiting midwife, that if things got worse, we needed to call the emergency helpline and say that Kate was almost at the stage where she was contemplating ending her life. Only then would the situation be treated with the seriousness it warranted.

This is unacceptable in my view. How can urgent action be delayed in this way? Why do people have to risk their sanity and in some cases lose their lives before something is done? Why had Kate not been referred early on in her pregnancy to the relevant professional who could have given us guidance on what to expect? Even now, I find this hard to come to terms with.

Yet again, the analogy of physical illness comes to mind. If someone is suffering from severe chest pains and shortness of breath, they are rushed to an accident and emergency department at the nearest hospital. Nobody questions their symptoms before they are examined and in most cases, rapid attention is given in order to pre-empt a further deterioration.

The world of mental health is so unfairly different. People's symptoms and pain are all too often not recognised and acknowledged with the same gravity as someone suffering from physical illness. Society has a different attitude to mental illness. Often, it can be a silent killer, as without diagnosis, the condition can be too advanced to revert. The injustice and disparity in our society induced me to start writing this book. I feel anger and resentment towards a society, which is neglecting to address the needs of the mentally ill.

Our biggest fear was the possibility of Kate being hospitalised. We informed the health workers of our wish to treat this from home, if possible. Luckily, we were given round the clock support.

I was so relieved to have my mother on hand as I knew she would be able to keep an eye on Kate and Maia whilst I was away at work. Kate could not be left alone, but she was unhappy with the situation. On the days that she felt better, she wanted her own space and told me that she could not be herself with my mother around. She felt as if she was entertaining someone when she least wanted to. She knew that my mother had the best intentions, but still she felt like a prisoner in her own home.

This period was the darkest in Kate's depression, but was also a turning point.

On one of many nights that I could not sleep, I decided to 'surf' the Internet to pass the time. I looked at news websites for quite a while but I was not really reading what was on the screen. I was just clicking aimlessly on links to websites. Between these cyber wanderings, I typed the word 'depression' into a search engine and was not surprised to get a huge number of hits. I started randomly opening some of them. One of the links gave me a poignant insight into depression. The idea was encapsulated in the following sentence: 'Depression is a disease of loss'. I read this sentence over and over again. How painfully true this was.

On a physiological level, Kate had lost her appetite, her ability to sleep, and think rationally. On an emotional level, the loss was immeasurable. Kate had lost her sense of security, confidence and self-esteem and at her worst period, her will to live. I had lost my ability to help her and protect her from these feelings.

In many ways, this feeling of loss was paradoxical to reality. We had been blessed with a beautiful and healthy daughter who was more than we could have ever hoped for. We had supportive family and friends, yet both of us felt so lonely and isolated. The house looked so happy with all the baby things, yet a feeling of sadness prevailed. Nothing was what it seemed or should have been. I felt robbed of what should have been an incredible milestone in our lives.

On the Mend

I cannot pinpoint the exact time when things started getting better. There was not a particular event that signalled the beginning of the road to recovery. Our previous experiences in dealing with Kate's depression showed that improvements were slow and gradual. We knew we had to be patient and persevere.

One of the first signs of improvement I saw, was when I came home one day after work to find Kate cuddling Maia, who had fallen asleep on her. Maia's tiny frame was curled up and her head was resting on Kate's chest. This is one of the most moving images I have of Maia in the first few months. Until then, Kate had struggled to bond with Maia and even to hold her. This was a turnaround. For the first time, I saw a look in Kate's eyes that showed that things were going to get better. There was an almost tactile bond between mother and child. It was as if opposite poles of two magnets had finally come together.

This was the image I had envisaged during the pregnancy and assumed was natural from birth. It was definitely a moment of breakthrough. For the first time in months, I felt we were turning the corner and looking at a brighter future. It had taken a few months to reach this stage, but it was worth the wait. Kate looked so much more at ease with herself and Maia.

When I asked if I could take Maia and give her a cuddle, Kate asked if I could wait, as she was so comfortable in that position. I was ecstatic and emotional at this response. Until now, Kate had usually been relieved to hand Maia over to me after being with her the entire day. Now, for the first time, she wanted to hold her more.

This was and is one of my most special memories. There is nothing more uplifting for a husband than to see his wife and child in complete harmony with each other. I was so proud of Kate for finally allowing herself to accept Maia's presence and to reciprocate her love. They had finally bonded. A very small part of me was actually envious of this intense bond. I wondered whether it was more natural or stronger than a bond between husband and wife. I also wondered if I would ever reach this level of closeness with Maia. As a man, it is hard to comprehend the mother-child bond, as biology dictates a very different role for us.

Another part of Kate's recovery was re-establishing a routine that was not focused entirely around Maia. I could not remember the last time Kate had had some time to herself, to do things that were simply for her benefit. As a couple, we had had very little time on our own.

I decided to take Kate shopping in town for the day. We left Maia with a friend and we had the day just to ourselves. When we left the house, we both felt a sense of guilt, but more than anything, a huge sense of relief. We were somewhat overwhelmed at our regained 'freedom', which we had taken for granted before Maia's birth.

It seemed as if we had a huge amount of time on our hands and this was awkward, yet wonderful. For the first time in months, we could actually spend the day doing very little, at our own pace, as and when we wanted. It felt very special to have a break from everyone and we were both reminded of the days of our courtship. We were on a date! It felt invigorating.

This day helped us both immeasurably. It made me realise the need to maintain our life as a couple, in addition to being a family. It is easy to be overwhelmed at being new parents and forget the need to develop and work at the partner relationship. After Maia's birth, the simplest activities such as shopping or going to the movies, seemed exciting, whereas beforehand we had taken these things for granted. We had started off as individuals who became a unit, which had now expanded to a family of three. However, each of these entities needed development and nurturing. Neither Kate nor I could be optimal spouses or parents without developing ourselves. This particular day reminded me of all Kate's wonderful qualities and made me appreciate her as a truly unique individual, wife and mother.

Kate is very creative and has a multitude of hobbies ranging from gardening to card making. The period after the birth had given her practically no time to herself. I knew that she was desperate for some quality time to do her own thing. I decided to make a concerted effort to take Maia for a few hours on a regular basis and allow Kate time to herself. One morning, Kate had the time to potter in the garden, something she had not done for months. It was imperative for Kate to feel that being a mother had not stripped her of her individuality or ability to pursue her hobbies. Immediately after the birth, it was difficult to imagine that either of us could enjoy some free time, but, as we developed more of a routine, we realised that it was possible.

As the weeks went by, Maia was more settled in her routine thanks to Kate's concerted efforts. We were very fortunate that Maia had very agreeable sleep patterns and after seven or eight weeks was sleeping through most of the night. This was a salvation for us. It allowed us to have regular hours of sleep at regular times of the day. It also allowed us to plan things more easily and relax.

One of the key factors in coping with the depression was to ensure that we had planned ahead as much as possible in order to avoid any unnecessary stress or pressure. We would always have Maia's bottles sterilised the night before for the next day, as well as a bag with all the essentials ready for Kate to take whenever she went out with her. This planning made things much easier. Sleep is essential to all, but for new parents, it is an indulgence. We took turns in looking after Maia on days when we both wanted a few hours of sleep or rest. This meant that we could have some quality, uninterrupted sleep.

As we became more organised, we started venturing out as a family on short day trips. This was also a turning point for us and especially for Kate, who had felt too scared and vulnerable to go out. I had also felt apprehensive about a day trip. As we went out more, our preparation time was quicker and we were more relaxed throughout the day.

There were days or moments when Kate suddenly felt very low and seemed to regress. Such is the nature of depression. We fought through those days and maintained a level of determination to get things on track. We knew that whatever happened, Kate's frame of mind was definitely improving. For the first time in months there were more good days than bad ones. It was a gradual process.

Kate told me that one day she felt that a light switch had been turned on in her mind and all of a sudden things started to get brighter. However, it was still important to remember that the situation could change without warning.

Much of her disposition was related to tiredness. Kate and lack of sleep do not go together. She needs her eight hours and is bad-tempered, suffering from migraines, if she loses sleep. Having Maia up every two hours was extremely hard for her and if she had looked after her during the night, she was not really alert until at least 2pm the next day. She once told me that what made her persevere, was the knowledge that millions of other women around the world were doing the same thing.

Why Kate?

One of the most fundamental concerns I had during this period, was to try and understand the root of the illness. What had caused the depression? Was it psychologically, environmentally or hormonally based? How could the miraculous and easy birth of a child have created such turmoil in my wonderful wife?

In an effort to try and understand the causes and reasons for our predicament, I started researching the causes of postnatal depression. There were so many conflicting theories of the causes of the illness. Unsurprisingly, I read that an average of one in seven women suffered from postnatal depression. This reassured me to a degree, and Kate felt that she was not an isolated case. It is also human nature to feel comforted by the fact that others are also suffering.

During Kate's pregnancy, we were told that in light of her past history of depression, there was a stronger likelihood she would suffer from postnatal depression. This had been a concern from the outset.

It angered Kate that her past history had been ignored at the antenatal visits. When she initially filled in a form after the 12 week scan, she wrote 'depression' in the pre-existing conditions section. It was there in black and white but was never once discussed.

When she was about 20 weeks pregnant Kate told the midwife at the hospital that she was concerned about getting postnatal depression. The midwife immediately went to see her superior and arranged for a counsellor to get in touch by letter. The letter or appointment never materialised. Just before the due date it transpired that the hospital had totally forgotten to alert the psychiatric team and at the last minute Kate had to rush around trying to get an emergency referral before the birth.

She had even read up about a progesterone or oestrogen injection that could be administered immediately after the placenta had been delivered, to counteract the rapid loss of hormones from the body. She requested further information about it from her GP and the midwives in the hospital, both of whom were unable to help. Consequently, Kate felt very let down and time was running out.

However, there was equal evidence to suggest that Kate may actually have no symptoms at all and that very often women who are usually sufferers of depression can actually bloom after giving birth. I was sceptical of the latter opinion as I could already see certain signs during the pregnancy that indicated a possible crisis in the future.

What surprised me most of all was that there was no conclusive evidence to suggest that postnatal depression in women was exclusively hormonal. There were opinions that held that it was just as attributable to psychosocial factors, such as too little or too much support, a sense of perceived adversity, irrational thoughts, fears and fantasies of the mother and child and general feelings of being out of control.

When I sat down and thought of Kate's symptoms throughout our relationship and after the birth of our daughter, they were more indicative of the psychosocial factors. The described symptoms seemed almost customised to match Kate. I could particularly identify with the sense of perceived adversity.

Kate had displayed an irrational sense of vulnerability and insecurity, worrying about finances, as she was not working. She also said that felt that she only had a few friends who really like her. Nothing was further from the truth. In reality, Kate was being smothered with affection from many different friends and was very much loved by them

She was critical about everything she did with Maia, continually berating herself. She felt she was useless and had lost control of her life, routine and individuality. These were all classic signs of postnatal depression.

Maia went through a stage of bringing up a whole feed after being fed. Kate felt that it only ever happened to her – and was convinced she was doing something wrong. Eventually she became too scared to feed her with the bottle and was secretly relieved when another family member offered to do a feed.

I learnt that there were three types of postnatal emotional disorders, each with increasing severity: postnatal blues, postnatal depression and anxiety and postnatal psychosis, or puerperal psychosis.

In the first few days after Maia's birth I prayed and hoped that Kate just had the blues. Unfortunately, things had deteriorated to a more serious scenario. I realised that Kate's symptoms of excessive dependency, hopelessness, numbness and loss of appetite were more like postnatal depression and anxiety.

What was the most distressing was, seeing Kate at her lowest point where I felt that she touched on the symptoms of postnatal psychosis. I remember seeing her totally disoriented and detached from her surroundings. She was barely responsive to people around her and seemed to have isolated herself emotionally and psychologically. I felt as if she was in another world, to which I had no access. It felt as if I was losing her. I was terrified indeed that I had no control over Kate's deterioration.

However, I had experienced Kate's previous bouts of

depression in the past few years and could make a comparison with her present state of mind. I knew this episode was different from the others. It was something much darker and ominous. I knew I had to call in the professionals and alert them to the severity of our situation. I am forever grateful for having been able to recognise the harshness of the depression and find help in curbing its malignant path of destruction.

The saving grace of the medical professionals was our new GP who had been recommended to us by friends. He had dealt with numerous cases of depression in his years of experience and had the sensitivity and professional expertise to make us believe things were going to get better. After registering with him, both Kate and I felt that for the first time in months, we were in the hands of someone who could help. Moreover, he addressed the problem as a joint problem, acknowledging that we were both suffering. It is not only the patients who suffer, but also their loved ones.

I shudder to think how much lower we could have fallen. We eluded the depths of despair by the tiniest of margins. My heart goes out to all who have not been fortunate enough to detect the problem in time or perhaps lacked the support system to help them deal with the depression. What fighting chance did they have of recovery? How could they avoid falling between the cracks of an ill-equipped health system?

What About Me?

"How are you coping? Four simple words. All I needed to hear was something along these lines.

Throughout this difficult period, we were surrounded by friends and family who would ask: "How is Kate doing?", yet there were very few people who actually thought of asking me how I was faring in this ordeal.

Kate once described to me an interesting scenario. She described it as a sort of pecking order. She said that when you are pregnant people just stare at your bump when they talk to you, a bit like a man staring at a woman's breasts when having a chat. You cease to exist and people see you as a walking bump. Then when the baby is born people just want to see the baby, presents are bought for the baby and the mother is occasionally referred to in passing conversation. The father might just as well not exist – his role becomes a silent and invisible tea and coffee maker for the mass of visitors, when in fact he is the one holding the fort.

With the exception of a couple of friends and my immediate family, there were very few mentions of me. I am not the kind of person who requires constant attention or recognition. However, as time passed on, I began to feel more resentful and angry with people, especially those closer to the real picture, for not acknowledging that I was also part of this nightmare.

There was a recurring scene of family members calling or visiting, ignoring me and going straight in to see how Kate or the baby were doing. I assumed that they thought that I was okay as I was functioning fine superficially and holding things together. I was working harder than ever and keeping a close eye on things at home too. If there was a problem at home, Kate knew she could call on me anytime and I would be on hand to help. Most of the time, I could talk her through an episode on the telephone, avoiding the need to come home.

I had become experienced in differentiating between a very bad day that would get worse, and a rough couple of hours. In many senses, we were able to assess these episodes together and acknowledge them for what they were at the time. This is something that is very helpful and necessary, not only to the person suffering depression, but also to those around them.

Whilst I did not expect every person to sympathise with what was happening, I did have expectations from those who knew .My mother was extremely concerned about the whole situation, as she saw first hand what was happening at home. I was coming home after a stressful day at work to Kate who had bravely attempted to put on her 'glad rags', both physically and mentally, during the day when visitors came. However, when I came home, the veil dropped and she needed me desperately to recharge her batteries and spend time alone with me. She also needed time away from the baby. I found myself bathing and feeding Maia, whilst Kate had a nap. After that I would make a light dinner and speak to Kate about how she was feeling. Unfortunately, on most days she was mentally and physically exhausted. The medication had started kicking in, but it also had the side effects of tiredness and lethargy. By the time dinner was over, we managed to speak briefly before Kate needed to go to bed again. I did the later 10.30pm feed, which allowed Kate to go to sleep until the early hours of the morning.

Kate's depression had also reduced her concentration span, so much so that when she sometimes called me at work, she forgot why she had called me. We usually retraced her thoughts until we managed to remember what she had though of in the first instance. I found this very difficult.

She also got lost in shops and started panicking. It first happened when she went shopping for food at the local supermarket. She called me saying that she could not remember what she went for. She sounded embarrassed and confused. At first I thought it quite funny and made a flippant comment about it. This was definitely not the correct response. Kate was upset and scared and felt as if she was losing her memory and common sense. I should have reassured her instead of dismissing the incident. On another occasion, she went to a nearby DIY shop to buy some paint. A couple of hours later and she had still not come back. I began to worry. Just as I was about to call her, she arrived home. She was very upset and said she found the whole thing very confusing, going round and round in circles in the paint section reading all the labels very slowly.

Of course I wanted to be there for Kate when I came home, but I was drained too. I also needed some time and attention. I began almost dreading coming home as I knew that this recurring scene was awaiting me. I felt as if I had been caught in a strong current at sea. Every time I managed to get my head just above water and regain my breath, another wave came and swept me back under. I was exhausted. I could see no respite to this continual struggle and was beginning to feel slightly numb myself.

I secretly longed for the days when it was just Kate and myself and I could just come home and relax without having to be on this constant treadmill. Everything now was centred around Kate and Maia. I had lost 'me' time and was neglecting myself.

I started comfort eating to distract me from the situation at home. I would come home, go the kitchen, and before I even sat down to have a meal, would eat a couple of chocolates, lots of bread and anything else tempting. I never actually put the food on a plate and sat down in a relaxed fashion, I just ate straight from the cupboard or the fridge. This was my way of pretending that I was eating less than I actually was. I rationalised it by saying to myself that I was just having some tasters of food before dinner.

I was unaware of the amount I was eating until my mother, who was still staying with us, came into the kitchen and remarked that I was eating too much, too quickly and on my own. I had become a secret lone eater. This was not a healthy sign. I was not even enjoying what I was eating, but simply devouring it. I knew it was unacceptable, but I was out of control. If a day had gone particularly badly, it would be reflected in my eating habits.

I also used to visit the local corner shop on the way home and treat myself to some sweet or chocolates, which I saw as a kind of pain reliever for what I was going through. My tendencies to comfort eat and allow myself to let go, came as a shock to my family. In the past, I had been very aware of correct eating habits and had exercised regularly. I took a lot of pride in and made an effort with my appearance. Since getting married, I had gained some weight, but nothing significant. I think many people tend to gain some weight after their marriage for various reasons, contentment, more social eating and more of a routine existence. I also think that living in a cold climate such as the UK, is not conducive to healthy eating, as it is common to crave food to keep warm.

Since Maia's birth I had put on at least ten kilograms, which definitely showed. In addition to my weight gain, I had a generally unhealthy look. My skin was sallow and grey and I had huge black rings under my eyes that seemed more accentuated with my bloated face. I remember sending some pictures of myself, Kate and Maia to my brothers abroad. When I spoke to my brother a few weeks later, he commented in the subtlest way possible that he had been shocked at how I looked and that I needed to take myself in hand. I felt and looked awful. I had also developed quite severe asthma as a result of my pollen and hay fever allergies, which were particularly bad at the time. I was using inhalers and taking medication to keep it under control, but was still very uncomfortable and found it difficult to breathe.

Sleeplessness overcame me. I found it very difficult to fall asleep at night and when I did, sleep was interrupted and light. I was constantly worrying about the situation: Was Kate going to get better? Were we going to cope financially and why was I feeling so low?

I lingered on in this numb state for a couple of weeks and convinced myself that I just needed to ride the storm. Kate was on medication, which was helping and she seemed to be turning the corner. This was no time to give up yet. Yes, I was tired and feeling low, but this was only natural and not something unexpected or extraordinary. At the time we had quite a few friends who had recently had babies and I knew there were others who found it difficult. I convinced myself that I was overreacting.

A week later, as my alarm sounded at 6am to get up for work, I could not move. I was frozen. I just could not get myself out of bed. My head felt like it had lead weights on it. I was immobile. I sat on the corner of the bed for what must have seemed ages but was probably no more than fifteen minutes and felt like a displaced person, disorientated and bewildered by my surroundings. I knew I had to get ready for work, but was physically unable to get myself ready. This was it. My batteries, which had been overloaded for a long time already, seemed finally drained of any energy.

I was shocked at how I felt. I could not believe that this was me. Something was definitely wrong. What would have normally taken about twenty minutes took almost two hours. Were my allergies and medication making me feel this way?

Later that morning, I decided to call my GP to discuss what had happened and get some advice. I told Kate that I was going beforehand, but yet again underplayed how I was really feeling. I had told Kate I was going to visit the GP and had alluded that it was not only my asthma that was bothering me, but also my state of mind. I did not want to over-emphasise the latter, as the last thing I wanted to do was make her feel guilty for the way I felt. As adults, we are accountable for our actions and need to take responsibility for ourselves.

I surprised myself at taking the initiative to make the appointment with the GP. I usually try to avoid the experience of going to the doctor at all costs. I am the first to admit that I am a very bad patient. When I do go, it is usually when I can no longer take the pain or when Kate has actually ordered me to go. However, on this occasion, I felt I had to go for the sake of Kate and Maia.

As I walked from my car to the doctor's surgery, the events of the last few months replayed in my head. I thought of the paradoxical feelings of having a wonderful wife and daughter coupled with all the difficulties and challenges we had experienced and I wondered why it could not have been simpler. I was determined to make myself feel better. I had to be as honest as possible with the doctor.

Our doctor was very sympathetic to the situation and as he had been seeing Kate, he was fully aware of how difficult things had been. I described what I was feeling, although he seemed to know that just by looking at me. I tried very hard to remain composed as possible throughout the conversation without sounding too self- pitying.

At the end of my account of how I was feeling, I felt a huge sense of relief. It was the first time I had actually taken the time to reflect and articulate what had happened in the past few months to an objective person who was emotionally detached from the situation.

Throughout my recall of events, the doctor looked at me intensely, yet with a sense of compassion. He told me that I had been through an ordeal with very little support and that in spite of all the difficulties, I had managed to keep things afloat both at home and at work. He confirmed that I was worn out and that my asthma was particularly bad because I was so run down. He recommended some time off work.

I was more concerned about taking time off work than anything he was telling me. It was a very busy period and I had been given more responsibility, which was flattering on the one hand, but at the same time prevented me from taking time off. I explained my concerns to the doctor who compromised with me and said I needed a minimum of one week to help my asthma and help me to switch off as much as possible.

As much as I hated admitting it, I had no choice. I was being a fool for prioritising my work over my personal health and family. I have always been loyal to my employers and I felt I was letting them down. Logically, this should not have concerned me, as my company were not the most appreciative people at the best of times. Nothing could have shocked me more than the next words he uttered: "You are showing classic signs of depression. I think you are at the beginning of a bout of depression."

I asked him to repeat what he had just said to make sure that I had heard correctly. I just could not fathom how this could have happened to me. I have never been depressed before and have always managed to keep on top of things, in spite of the various setbacks I have had over the years.

For the first time in my life, I could really empathise with someone who suffered from depression from first hand experience. Despite my open-mindedness, I dare say that I felt embarrassed for being another 'depression' statistic. I felt I was now on the verge of being trapped in a dark world by this monster of depression, which seemed to devour the happiness and mental well being of so many people. I did not want to be part of this world and wanted to be an outsider looking in. Yet I was angry with myself for feeling like this. I had thought that I was non-judgemental, but this response indicated that, subliminally, I still had some prejudices about mental illness.

I kept on asking the doctor if he was sure I was suffering from depression. I was hoping he would say it was something else.

I needed to internalise this reality and work out a strategy to overcome it while it was still in its inception. I was determined not to become another statistic and did not entertain the thought of being out of action for too long. I had to be strong for Kate and Maia. If I cracked, who would look after them? I did not dare contemplate those thoughts.

Reality had caught up with me. My endurance levels had been pushed to extremes. I was lucky that I was able to realise that something was wrong and seek help. If I had not gone to the doctor, I would have probably cracked. I informed the doctor that I would discuss it with Kate before giving a final answer.

When I got home, I explained the situation to Kate. She was angry and upset by the situation. Angry at me for not looking out more for myself and being too loyal to my work, and upset that she had caused my decline.

"It's all my fault. I am a rubbish wife. You deserve someone better."

Kate was convinced that my frame of mind was her fault – she said that if she did not exist, then none of this would have happened. She told me that she felt very guilty and upset about how I was feeling.

Of course, it was not her fault. We were submerged by a very trying situation. My experience has shown that it is quite unusual for both partners in a relationship to be equally fulfilled personally and professionally. In our relationship, one of us always seemed to be feeling better or in a better job than the other. We have never been in a situation where we both felt that we were in fulfilling, successful jobs.

I also kept on reminding Kate that during our lives, there would be times when I would need her to carry me and I knew that she would undoubtedly be there for me.

In hindsight, I think that the doctor's warning of my symptoms of depression, was a wake-up call for Kate. It made her realise that anyone could be affected by depression and it was not something that only sensitive people like her had to endure. It also shocked her as she saw the toll the last few months had had on me. This gave Kate more motivation to make every effort to try to feel more optimistic about the future and her well-being.

Depression is also about self-healing to a large extent. Medication and treatment can and do provide essential tools for coping with depression, but the sufferer has the monumental task of battling with the illness and finding the inner strength and courage to overcome it, for their own sake and those around them.

Kate was scared that I was going to leave her. I had to go back to work, as I did not have very much leave.

Kate said she felt that I was returning to work prematurely as a form of escapism. She also felt that when I came home, it seemed that I was reluctant to be with her. This was not the case. Of course, it was difficult at home, but at the same time I wanted to be there as much as possible in order to support both Kate and Maia.

In many ways, work was a form of escapism and a safety net for me. It did not allow me the luxury of wallowing in self-pity or worrying about our situation. Instead it gave me a sense of focus and direction and reminded me that life is about coping with situations and getting on with things. One cannot always overcome troubles easily, but one can certainly continue to live. This is what I was trying to achieve.

Kate became paranoid every time I was on the telephone to my family. She was convinced that she had heard me whispering about how I wanted to leave her and how unhappy I was in the relationship. I was unhappy with the situation but this was not anyone's fault. My pain was not caused by Kate, yet she found this very difficult to comprehend. She felt there was a real feeling of anger in the air and was very scared, as she felt so vulnerable.

I did indeed discuss the situation with my family, but this was my legitimate right. I needed to relay the situation and update them on how things were going. Kate found it difficult to accept that these discussions were a channel for me to try and understand what she was going through and provide some sort of support.

I had an old school friend, Jonathan who suffered from depression in his early twenties. We had lost touch over the years and one day I heard that he had committed suicide. I could not believe that he had felt so desperate and helpless that he needed to resort to such a tragic action.

Jonathan had a supportive circle of friends and family. I remember visiting his parents a few weeks after his death. They had known me from when I was in pre-school and were touched that I had come. During the visit, Jonathan's mother mentioned to me that he had been on medication and had had numerous sessions of therapy. However, I subsequently found out that while he had been on medication, he had felt that there was little point continuing to battle his illness. He had not been particularly lucky in love or in his career. He began to lose hope in getting better.

Hope is a gift that can provide a lifeline for a person throughout life's ups and downs. It gives us strength when we think we have none left, and gives us resolve when there may seem to be no point in continuing. Once hope is gone, it is almost impossible to salvage oneself from the depths of despair. I realised that Jonathan had lost that hope and with it, his battle for life.

In our case, Kate and I still had the gift of hope, as we knew there was so much to look forward to in the life that we were building together. I am not sure how things would have turned out if we had been going through this alone.

Getting Better

Optimism. Perseverance. These were two words I tried to internalise following my visit to the doctor. I had to start seeing and feeling the positive things that were in my life.

Kate and I decided to go away to a country lodge for two days in order to allow us to assess our situation and have some time out from what had been a harrowing few months. Maia came along with us. It was our first mini holiday together. Kate actually booked the holiday as a surprise as she wanted to kick start my recovery and have some quality time together.

It turned out to be one of the best holidays we have ever had. It gave us time to see things from a different perspective as we extricated ourselves temporarily from the mundane routine we were accustomed to.

At first, I was somewhat apprehensive about going on holiday with Maia. As much as I adore everything about her, I was advised by the doctor to have total rest and I was concerned that we would simply be transferring our routine from home to a country lodge, which would defeat the purpose. I had even considered going away on my own to see my family abroad. However, I felt that I could not and did not want to leave my two ladies who were also going through a difficult time. Kate was also desperate for a break and it was unthinkable to leave her on her own with Maia.

Maia was very well behaved throughout the holiday and made Kate and I appreciate even more what a gift she is. My favourite and most special moment was when we took Maia swimming. This is the first truly happy family moment, which is etched in my memory.

Kate and I unwrapped little Maia from her various layers of clothing and dressed her in a two-tone, pink swimming costume with a butterfly motif. We both carried her into the water and allowed her to glide onto the water. She was initially confused – why were so many other people in her bath? However, after a few minutes, she had immersed herself in the water and was having a wonderful time.

I lifted her high and held her little body in the air while her feet kicked about energetically. She looked at me with a radiant smile and chuckled in delight. I felt more bonded with her than ever. As I carried her in the water, I held her tightly to my chest, making sure to protect her. I was reminded more and more of the huge responsibility I had of protecting her from life's harsh elements.

I was equally enamoured by Kate who gave Maia so much love and attention. After Maia's swim, Kate dried and polished Maia, as if she was caring for a precious ornament.

For the rest of the holiday, we walked, swam and saw some breathtaking views in the surrounding lakes and mountains. We both felt as if a pause button had been pressed and we could escape reality for just a few days.

We managed to talk extensively to one another, something we had not properly done for quite some time. I was still weak, fatigued and suffering quite badly from my asthma, but was still able to relax and enjoy the time out.

Despite some significant improvement during these few days, one incident occurred, which reminded us both that we were still not out of the woods. We had stopped on the way home at a shopping centre. I was the only one with a mobile telephone, as Kate had left hers, together with her wallet, in the car. All she had in her possession was Maia strapped in a pouch. I told Kate I was just going to pop into a clothes shop for a few minutes and would be back to meet her and Maia in a nearby shop.

As it turned out, there was quite a queue for the tills and I was about ten minutes late. As I walked back towards where Kate had been, I saw someone in the distance who resembled Kate, but she was crying. As I came closer, I realised that it was Kate. What had happened in the few minutes I had been away?

"I thought that you had run away from me and Maia or that you had been kidnapped", The crying continued. At first my reaction was rather nonchalant.

"Of course I wouldn't leave you. How could you think that?" I was rather surprised by how Kate could have surmised that I would do this. Kate continued to cry and answered:

"But you were ten minutes late. I thought you had left me – I had absolutely no way of contacting you."

Under normal circumstances, Kate would never have been so sensitive about me being slightly late. I omitted to take into account her fragile state of mind when I decided to remain in the queue and return slightly later than the agreed time. This was a mistake. After a lengthy discussion, I apologised for the worry I had caused. This incident made me realise that someone coming out of a depression can still have setbacks and will still be more sensitive than usual in certain situations.

We discussed working out an action plan to get back on track. My first resolution was to begin making efforts to take control of my eating habits. I had also not exercised in months and decided to cut down on the junk food I was eating and resume an exercise regime. I have always loved swimming and had previously swum every day. On our return home, I vowed to resume my gym membership and take some time out to exercise, to burn off the stress and calories too.

My road to recovery on the eating front was much more difficult. I was realistic about taking drastic measures and knew this would take a significant period of time. I was not quite ready for a rigorous diet regime. I decided to gradually take more care of what I was eating and cut down slowly on some of the more unhealthy foods I was eating.

Another issue was dealing with the anger and resentment I was harbouring towards Kate's family, particularly her mother, whom I felt had been a good mother to her daughter, but insensitive to me as her daughter's husband. I felt that she saw my role in life as making her daughter happy and that my needs and feelings were secondary to fulfilling that role. In many ways, that is probably quite a natural feeling. Becoming a mother-in-law is also difficult, and I am not the non-opinionated person who tows the line. I have always been vocal and expressive of my views and do not just agree for the sake of diplomacy. My mother-in-law is also a strong personality and probably found me quite of a challenge.

During this period, my mother had observed that I

was seemingly neglected and also in need of support, and was disappointed that there seemed to be little concern for my needs. She mentioned this to my mother-in-law and the discussion, which followed, was quite unpleasant.

I think this came as a shock to my mother-in law who until then, had not realised that I was suffering too. In some senses, she probably felt quite embarrassed about the situation and did not want to talk to me directly about it. Instead, she asked her partner to talk to me, but this offended me even further. I felt that there was an inherent breakdown of communication between us, and that for some reason she felt that she could not really approach it head on. Instead, she chose to ignore it, hoping that things would get better.

They did not. In fact, they only got worse. What ensued was a period of several weeks in which my mother in-law called Kate when I was not at home and avoided speaking with me.

I decided that if I was to resume a healthy, open relationship again with Kate's mother, I needed to be more open about the situation. I knew this was not going to be easy. However, I was not prepared to lie to myself or anyone else about how I was feeling. I had discussed this with Kate, who understood and sympathised with my point of view, but did not want to intervene. I understood this and did not want to add additional stress to what was already a difficult period.

I asked my mother-in-law to meet me at a park to talk about the situation. It was very difficult for me as I did not want a confrontation and did not have the energy to have an argument. However, I felt that it was imperative to my healing process to sort out our problems, in order to avoid a recurrence. I reiterated to her that I was approaching the subject with the intention of wanting to resolve matters, as I valued the good relationship I had with her. I knew that she would do anything for her children and was absolutely devoted to them. I just wanted to remind her that if I was unhappy, this would affect Kate and our relationship too.

After several hours of debating, she acknowledged that she had underestimated what I had been through. This had not been out of any ill intention, but because she had been preoccupied with Kate's situation. I did not get an apology and was not really looking for one. All I wanted and have ever wanted was an acknowledgement of my pain and some empathy.

Our relationship resumed on a much more positive note and she made a huge effort to restore it to what it had been before. The relationship is not perfect, but I think this episode was a turning point. It made me realise that I needed to be more open about issues I was facing with Kate's family and particularly her mother. It also made them realise that I would need to be considered more in the future and that Kate's happiness was inevitably intertwined with mine. If either of us was down, it would impact on the relationship.

This incident also reminded me of my two biggest faults. The first one being that I have always had very high standards of people I care about and get bitterly disappointed if I feel someone has not met them. I expect people to think the way I do, which is simply not going to happen. I need to accept that people have different ways of dealing with things and that they can make mistakes.

My second fault is my tendency to keep issues bottled inside and not discuss them until I am on the verge of exploding. The result is that what may start out as a relatively uncomplicated matter can turn into a monumental argument. I have always been poor at communicating in this way, particularly with family, but oddly enough, I can articulate my feelings eloquently to people I am not close to.

I made a resolution to try harder on this front and actually let people try and help me. I have never been very good at asking or receiving help and have felt better about giving it. There is nothing weak or sad in actually asking for it as on the most part people actually want to help. If one doesn't voice a request for help, they shouldn't be disappointed if it doesn't come. In my case, I assessed the situation by my high standards. I expected people to acknowledge the problem and offer help without me having to ask for it. My mistake was in assuming that people actually knew there was a problem.

Light at Last

My story is not one of despair and pain. Whilst those elements have certainly been prevalent at various stages, the ultimate message I wish to convey is a positive one. My experiences with Kate's depression have reinforced my views that people are indeed much stronger than they think, and have the resilience to overcome emotional hurdles they never thought they could or would experience. Not only can you overcome them, but you can become a stronger and better person too.

I did not always feel positive about the future. There were moments when my emotional and physical strength were very low. I had no indication of whether the ordeal had become a way of life, or whether it was a transient phase. I was envious at times, of acquaintances with their stable routines, which did not fluctuate according to state of mind.

I felt that we were subject to the wrath of the silent 'third partner' in our marriage. It was this partner who could arbitrarily decide whether the day was going to be bearable or whether it was going to be fraught with pain and uncertainty. We had no control over the timing and duration of the challenges we were presented with.

We had involuntarily been plunged into a challenge of a lifetime that seemed to have no set duration or intensity. There was very little we could do to prepare ourselves for what lay ahead and we knew nothing about the location or intensity of the hurdles along the course.

However, once the challenge seemed to have peaked, we were able to see the future from a more positive perspective. Kate and I both felt that the worst was over and we could now prepare to truly enjoy Maia.

Kate's confidence as a mother increased significantly as she realised that whatever she was doing, it was working. Maia is a delightful baby, who oozes happiness and contentment. She constantly smiles and coos and is extremely responsive to those around her. The credit for her disposition lies with Kate, who has passed on her sensitive and caring nature. Maia's placid disposition also refutes any theories about the negative affects of depression and postnatal depression on a newborn baby. Maia is truly contented and carefree and seems blissfully unaware of the difficult months surrounding her birth.

There is one occasion that remains etched in my memory as a day when I felt that Kate, Maia and I were truly over the ordeal of the depression. This was a day when all of life's worries and troubles were put aside and we were allowed a hiatus to enjoy what was a perfect day. It was a bank holiday in August and we had decided to go for the day to Formby, a stunning beach in a conservation area about fifty miles from our home. It was a mild summer's day and Kate and I were eager to leave the house and routine and enjoy a change of scene. I have always loved the sea and expanses of water in general. In many ways, they seem to be an escape for me. I can stare at them endlessly and work through my thoughts and feelings without having to say one word.

Before I met Kate, I had lived near the sea and would go regularly at the weekend for a brisk morning walk along the promenade in order to get some fresh air and exercise. I liked to go alone, preferring a Walkman and some music for company, to allow myself time to think thorough my thoughts over the past week. I had always found this more therapeutic and relaxing than any discussions I may have had with others. I was keen to go to the beach for the day as I hoped it would give me a sense of closure to the past few months.

Formby, like other beaches in the UK, is unusual in that it is not accessible or visible from the road, Instead, it requires one to park some distance away and walk towards it for quite some time. To me, this makes the beach and sea so much more alluring. As we arrived at the beach area, we noticed that the path to the beach itself was not very conducive to taking a four month old baby in a pram and that we would need to carry Maia for quite a bit of the journey.

We were not deterred, as we both knew that once we had made it to the harder sand, we could push Maia along. We shared the carrying of the pram and Maia and eventually made it to the beach. The view was breathtaking and definitely worth the initial difficulty in accessing it. We had to pass through a long corridor of dunes decorated with random infusions of greenery. The passage then widened and led to a colossal mass of wild blue sea. It was breathtaking. Looking back on this moment, the journey to the beach was symbolic of our journey over the past few months.

However, now we had finally reached a point where we could see further than the corridor and could appreciate what lay ahead of us. For the first time in months, I felt a sense of true happiness and optimism about the future. We had so much to look forward to and could appreciate life more now, having experienced the depths of desperation and fear. Without having to utter a word, Kate and I looked at each other, held hands and stopped in our tracks. For the next few minutes, we just stared at the view.

We decided to walk right along the water with Maia, as the sand there was very firm and we could quite easily push the pram. It was a particularly windy summer's day. The howling of the wind seemed to block out any other noises and in many ways made us feel more at ease with nature. We walked in the direction of the wind for at least an hour and I remember seeing Maia squeal with happiness as the wind blew in her face. For some reason, she loved the salty sea air. Her entire face lit up and she released an exuberant chuckle of delight. We all felt at ease with the wind pushing us forward and easing our walk along the beach. Finally, we decided to head back to where we had started. The return journey was an entirely different experience, as the very same wind that had aided us in our walk, was now working against us, making the walk much more challenging.

Even though we found this difficult, we persevered. When Kate was tired, I pushed Maia and vice versa. We could see in the far distance the place where we had started walking from and we both knew that with every step we made, we were closer to getting back home. This kept us going. We eventually arrived, slightly exasperated, but absolutely rejuvenated. It had been a cathartic experience for all of us. We finally had some closure and could look forward to the future.

Epilogue

My writing has not come without pain or difficulty. I have attempted to be brutally honest without holding back on some of the most trying moments that I have dealt with. My objective in writing this book was to be true to myself and to my experiences. I initially wrote down my thoughts in an attempt to make some sense of the disorder in my mind. I struggled to vocalise my thoughts to myself and others. The only way I could even begin to express myself, was through a frenetic brainstorm of what I was feeling and what I thought had led to the current situation. Any aberrations from the truth would only mislead and distort the realities of depression.

Whilst my initial thoughts seemed to reflect negativity and a burdened soul, as I started tracing back to the events that led to me meeting Kate, I was filled with a warm sensation. I began to focus on how much I loved her and the reasons I had fallen in love with her. I thought of our courtship, our travels and my marriage proposal. There had been so many incredible moments. I thought of how lucky we were to have had a daughter who seems to encapsulate the very essence of happiness and contentment. I thought of all these blessings. This process of introspection and appraisal was the most enlightening form of therapy I could have wished for. It gave my story perspective and the positive angle that needed to be shared with other people in similar situations. I was not going to allow these difficult times to erase the strength and commitment of our relationship.

Kate and I have not had closure with depression or its affect on our relationship. We have come through and tackled the obstacles, sometimes more successfully than others. I could not say that this has made our lives or marriage easier. However, it has bonded us more closely and reaffirmed our commitment to each other.

On a personal level, I have learnt so many life lessons. Firstly, I am aware of the need to express and vocalise my feelings to Kate, our families and friends. I felt guilty about telling Kate how I was being affected by her depression and I did not want her to feel that I was blaming her. I should have mentioned it at an earlier stage. This could have helped Kate behave differently. People do not necessarily know whether a person is suffering from depression. In our instance, most people were practically unaware as it was covered up. My mistake was in thinking that people actually knew what we were going through. I was absolutely wrong.

I have also learnt that I need to take time out for

myself and develop my interests and hobbies. A person's identity can be lost if he is multi-tasking as a father, husband, and son. My mistake was neglecting myself, and my need for self-development. I lost touch with my own feelings and what I wanted in life. Sometimes, I need to switch off from everything and everyone and spend time alone. I cannot honestly say that I am fully back on track in terms of making an effort to look after myself. I still need to eat less and exercise more and revert to the healthier lifestyle that I had several years ago. However, I am aware of my shortcomings in this area and this is probably one step closer to making a resolution to change.

My tendency to overwork at the expense of spending time with my family also needs to improve. I still find it difficult to juggle the needs of work with those on the home front. However, the best antidote for this weakness is when I see Maia. My routine on arriving home is that I say hello to, and then kiss Maia and I lift her high in the air. Her chuckles of laughter melt away the day's stresses. This is the most effective tonic and gives me some perspective on life. I have only recently managed not to look at work whatsoever for an entire day at the weekend. I have convinced myself that whatever it is, it can wait and will wait. I am slowly beginning to internalise the transience of human life and how life can pass us so quickly without having had time to appreciate the special moments. I am trying as much as possible to implement this philosophy into my life.

Asking for help is not a sign of weakness. Ideally, one

would hope that help is offered in some instances, particularly from those closest to the situation. Unfortunately, this is not always the case. People can be preoccupied with their own problems and only notice something is wrong at a very advanced stage.

More than anything, suffering alone is not only unnecessary, but also wrong. There are many silent sufferers of depression in a relationship, who internalise their feelings, often making matters more extreme when they are expressed. If one feels that they cannot speak to a close friend about the situation, they need to get professional help. These situations are complex and very often recurrent, requiring realistic and pragmatic strategies. Without this guidance, people can fall apart.

I have learnt to cherish my wife more than ever after experiencing the pain and torment endured in coping with depression, particularly in the process before and after the birth. I can now truly appreciate the monumental task women have of bringing children into this world and the effects this can have on them on an emotional, psychological and physiological basis. I do not take fatherhood or 'couple-hood' for granted and am aware of the continual need to work on these relationships for the rest of my life.

I can appreciate, more than ever, the joy children can bring into one's life. In the short span of Maia's life, we have had the pleasure of seeing her develop into a truly wonderful personality. Whilst we still feel a sense of numbness and pain over missing out on enjoying the first few months of her life, we have been given surplus dosages of joy in the subsequent period. We have laughed as a family as she ate her first solid food, shown us her first tooth and started to crawl. As each stage ends, another one begins that leaves us looking forward to the years ahead that we have together.

A friend recently asked me if we would go through this again. Six months ago I would have had difficulty answering that question. At the time, I couldn't appreciate the true bliss of parenthood. All I could focus on were the difficult changes, the effects on our relationship and the difficulties we subsequently experienced. Today, my answer would be, that if need be we would go through the same experience yet again. I would like to hope and believe that we would be much better equipped to deal with the situation and try as much as possible to pre-empt some of the problems. However, as with anything in life, there are no guarantees of being adequately prepared as we could face new issues not experienced before.

I cannot say I am not afraid or apprehensive about a recurrence of Kate's postnatal depression. However, I do know that there are an inordinate amount of factors, which could result in the experience recurring or not. Some of these are within our realm whilst others or not. I can only attempt, together with Kate, to face up to the issues and honestly as possible and provide each other with the support to deal with life's hurdles.

Kate has also learnt to be more aware of changes in my mood. My brush with depression has made her more aware than ever of the possibility of anyone falling prey to this illness at some stage in their lives. She also realised that part of the road to recovery was being able to reflect on the effects of depression on our loved ones. This provided a source of strength and perseverance when they she thought there were none left to give.

I have come to terms with the fact that there are no 'quick fixes' for dealing with depression. However, many, many people overcome it and lead productive lives. The most crucial coping mechanism is communication. Being able to express and acknowledge one's feelings is the key to helping ourselves and others. Kate has continued to deal with her depression through medication as well as other therapeutic channels such as art classes with people who also suffer from mental illness. These have been particularly useful in allowing her time to herself. Kate has also resumed work on freelance basis, which is one of the best things she could have done for her recovery. We both know how important it is to maintain one's sense of independence and develop oneself not only as a parent, but as an individual. Having a job makes you feel part of society and greatly increases your self-esteem.

Finally, we all need hope and optimism to get through life. In the darkest hours, I have always told myself to draw a line under some days and simply acknowledge that they have been unbearable without too much analysis and dissection of events. Each new day brings a new opportunity for change and this drives me to attempt, as best I can, to wake up with an open, optimistic frame of mind. This is my biggest challenge in life.